INSTANT REFERENCE

SPORTS

 TEACH YOURSELF®

For UK orders: please contact Bookpoint Ltd., 130 Milton Park, Abingdon, Oxon 0X14 4SB. Telephone: (44) 01235 827720. Fax: (44) 01235 400454. Lines are open from 09.00–18.00, Monday to Saturday, with a 24-hour message answering service. E:mail address: orders@bookpoint.co.uk

For U.S.A. order enquiries: please contact McGraw-Hill Customer Services, P.O. Box 545, Blacklick, OH 43004-0545, U.S.A. Telephone: 1-800-722-4726. Fax: 1-614-755-5645.

For Canada order enquiries: please contact McGraw-Hill Ryerson Ltd., 300 Water St, Whitby, Ontario L1N 9B6, Canada. Telephone: 905 430 5000. Fax: 905 430 5020.

Long renowned as the authoritative source for self-guided learning – with more than 30 million copies sold worldwide – the *Teach Yourself* series includes over 300 titles in the fields of languages, crafts, hobbies, business and education.

British Library Cataloguing in Publication Data
A catalogue record for this title is available from The British Library.

Library of Congress Catalog Card Number: On file

First published in UK 2001 by Hodder Headline Plc., 338 Euston Road, London, NW1 3BH.

First published in US 2001 by Contemporary Books, A Division of The McGraw-Hill Companies, 4255 West Touhy Avenue, Lincolnwood (Chicago), Illinois 60712-1975 U.S.A.

The 'Teach Yourself' name and logo are registered trade marks of Hodder & Stoughton Ltd.

Picture Credits:
With thanks to Popperfoto:
4, 7, 20, 54, 61, 67, 68, 70, 79, 81, 87, 102, 104. 111, 123, 137, 139, 141, 148, 156, 165, 168, 176
And AKG:
55, 94, 128, 138
All illustrations copyright Helicon Publishing Ltd.
Text Editor: Tracey Kifford
Typeset by TechType, Abingdon, Oxon
Printed in Great Britain for Hodder & Stoughton Educational, a division of Hodder Headline Plc, 338 Euston Road, London NW1 3BH by Cox & Wyman Ltd., Reading, Berkshire.

Impression number   10 9 8 7 6 5 4 3 2 1
Year   2007   2006   2005   2004   2003   2002   2001

Contents

Bold type in the text indicates a cross reference. A plural, or possessive, is given as the cross reference, i.e. is in bold type, even if the entry to which it refers is singular.

AAA (Amateur Athletics Association)

Founded in 1880, the AAA was the former English governing body for men's athletics. It has now been incorporated within the BAF (British Athletics Federation), which was founded in 1991. The British Athletics Federation was replaced in February 1999 by a new organization, UK Athletics, as the sport's governing body.

Aberdeen FC

Formed in 1903 when three local clubs – Orion, Victoria United, and Aberdeen United – amalgamated, Aberdeen had to wait 44 years for their first trophy, when they won the Scottish Cup in 1947. They won the League championship in 1954–55. The 1967 season saw them first play in Europe. Honours include the Cup Winners' Cup, Super Cup, Scottish League and Premier League (four times), Scottish Cup (seven times), Scottish League Cup (five times, and an unofficial League cup in 1945–6), and other assorted silverware.

Adidas

Formed in 1925 by Adolf 'Adi' Dassler, Adidas began life as a manufacturer of soccer boots and running shoes. The company is now the world's second largest sporting goods supplier (after **Nike**). The family is heavily involved in sportswear – Adolf's brother, Horst, founded rivals sports goods company Puma and a grandson, Adi Junior, has also launched an adventure shoe company. Adidas currently sponsors the **All Blacks** rugby union side and has individual sponsorship deals with many of the world's top footballers and athletes.

Admiral's Cup

The Admiral's Cup is a sailing tournament that was first held in 1957 and is held biennially. National teams consisting of three boats compete over three inshore courses (in the Solent, off the English coast) and three offshore courses culminating with the Fastnet race (established 1925), which is 973 km/605 mi long.

aerobics

A system of vigorous exercise, often incorporating dance elements, that is designed to improve the efficiency and performance of the body's cardiovascular system (heart and lungs). Aerobics classes are often high impact and can put a lot of strain on the body. Lower impact aerobic exercises that are less punishing to the joints and cause fewer sports related injuries include swimming, cycling, and race-walking. To be beneficial the exerciser should work to raise his heartbeat for at least 20 minutes three times per week.

> 6 If you are fit you don't need it; if you're not you shouldn't risk it. 9
>
> **Henry Ford**, on exercise.

Agostini, Giacomo (1943–   )

Italian motorcyclist who won a record 122 grand prix and 15 world titles. His world titles were at 350cc and 500cc and he was five times a dual champion. He won the **Isle of Man TT** (Tourist Trophy) ten times, a figure only bettered by Mike Hailwood and Joey Dunlop.

aikido (martial art)

Created by Morihei Ueshiba (1883–1969), aikido is the Japanese art of self-defence (*Budo* or 'martial way'). Many of the twisting and throwing techniques of aikido are derived from the samurai skills of **jujitsu**, while the striking techniques made with the open palm are similar to those used in **karate**. Two main systems of aikido are *uyeshiba*, which is primarily defensive, and *tomiki*, which has developed into a competitive sport. Aikido is promoted throughout the world by the Aikikai Foundation, founded in 1948.

Aintree

Located on the outskirts of Liverpool, northwest England, Aintree is the racecourse that hosts **The Grand National** steeplechase (established in 1839) every spring. There is also a car-racing circuit, used only for club racing. The British Grand Prix was held at Aintree in 1955, 1957, 1959, and 1961–62.

Alexeev, Vasiliy (1942–)

Soviet weightlifter who broke 80 world records between 1970 and 1977, a record for any sport. He was Olympic super-heavyweight champion twice, world champion seven times, and European champion on eight occasions. At one time the most decorated man in the USSR, he was regarded as the strongest man in the world. He carried the Soviet flag at the 1980 Moscow Olympics opening ceremony, but retired shortly afterwards.

Ali, Muhammad (1942–)

Adopted name of Cassius Marcellus Clay Jr, US boxer. Olympic light-heavyweight champion in 1960, he went on to become world professional heavyweight champion in 1964, and was the only man to regain the title twice. In December 1999, he was voted the British Broadcasting Corporation (BBC) 'Sports Personality of the Century', and the US magazine *Sports Illustrated* and the US newspaper *USA Today* both named him 'Sportsman of the Century'. Having had his title stripped from him in 1967 for refusing to be drafted into the US Army, he regained the title in 1974, lost it in February 1978, and regained it seven months later.

> ❝ It's just a job. Grass grows, birds fly, waves pound the sand. I beat people up. ❞
>
> **Muhammad Ali**, *New York Times*, 6 April 1977.

All Blacks, The

Nickname of the New Zealand international rugby union team, derived from their playing strip of black shirts (with a silver fern crest), shorts, and socks. The first New Zealand test side played in 1884 (in blue shirts with a gold fern!), though the All Blacks were born in 1893 when the New Zealand Rugby Football Union sent a touring team to Australia, and since then they have toured all major (and most minor) rugby-play-

All Blacks *The New Zealand All Blacks perform their traditional pre-match* Haka, *a war dance laying down a challenge to the opposing team.*

ing countries. Arguably the dominant rugby nation of the 20th century and winners of the inaugural 1987 World Cup, great All Blacks include Colin Meads, Kel Tremain, Wayne Shelford, Don Clarke, Andrew Mehrtens, and Jonah **Lomu**. Touring All Black sides often perform the *Haka*, a Maori war dance laying down a challenge to their opponents.

Alpine Club
Society formed in 1857–58 to promote mountaineering, not only in the Alps, but also throughout the world. It laid the foundations of Alpine literature in 1859 with the publication of *Peaks, Passes, and Glaciers*, under the editorship of John Ball. In 1863 it began to publish the *Alpine Journal*, which gives accounts of climbs and explorations by members of the club and now has an international reputation. In consort with the Royal Geographical Society the Alpine Club has sponsored numerous Everest expeditions since the 1920s.

amateur
(Latin *amare* 'to love') A person who pursues an activity or practises a sport for pleasure and not professionally for financial gain.

America's Cup
International yacht-racing trophy. The US schooner *America* was the winner of the Hundred Guinea Cup, a race around the Isle of

Wight organized by the Royal Yacht Squadron of Great Britain in 1851. Following this victory the cup was renamed the America's Cup and donated to the New York Yacht Club. An international challenge competition was started. It is now a seven-race series between two boats: one defending champion boat and one challenging. A preliminary competition, the Louis Vuitton Cup, is held to determine which boat will challenge the defending champion in the America's Cup. The USA monopolized the race until 1983, when an Australian crew won the trophy. All races were held at Newport, Rhode Island, until 1987 when the Perth Yacht Club, Australia, hosted the series. In 2000, the defending champions, New Zealand, defeated the Italian Prada syndicate. It was the first time that a nation other than the USA has won the America's Cup in consecutive years, as well as the first time that there was no US competitor in the final.

Apartheid, sporting boycotts

The racial segregation policy of the South African government from 1948 to 1994, which withheld full rights of citizenship from non-whites. By 1994 blacks and other racial groups had been given the right to vote and elections brought to power the first black president, Nelson Mandela. International sanctions against apartheid included sporting boycotts, which saw South Africa banned from participation in the **Olympics** and football **World Cup** and not invited to play in the first two **Rugby World Cups**. But the **British Lions** and France toured during the 1960s, 70s and 1980s, and though England's cricketers did not play official tests in South Africa, 'rebel' tours (as well as rebel rugby tours by the New Zealand Cavaliers and a European rugby squad) gave some pretence of international competition. The lack of international competition was a factor, albeit

> ❝ Whoever says sport and politics do not mix is silly and vicious. They can no longer be kept apart. ❞
>
> **Arthur Ashe**, US tennis player, 1970.

small, in the pressure to liberalize South Africa and in 1995 the country played host to the Rugby World Cup, winning the tournament. **See also:** *Springboks, The.*

Arc de Triomphe, Prix de l'
French horse race run over 2,400 m/1.5 miles at Longchamp, near Paris. It is the leading 'open age' race in Europe, and one of the richest. It was first run in 1920.

Archer, Frederick (1857–1886)
English jockey. He rode 2,748 winners in 8,084 races between 1870 and 1886, including 21 classic winners. He was a champion jockey 13 times between 1874 and 1886.

He won the Derby five times, the Oaks four times, the St Leger six times, the Two Thousand Guineas four times, and the One Thousand Guineas twice. He rode 246 winners in the 1885 season, a record that stood until 1933. Archer shot himself in a fit of depression.

archery
Originally used for hunting and warfare, and now a competitive sport, archery is the use of the bow and arrow to hit targets. The world governing body is the Fédération Internationale de Tir à l'Arc (FITA) founded 1931. Archery was reintroduced to the 1972 **Olympic Games**.

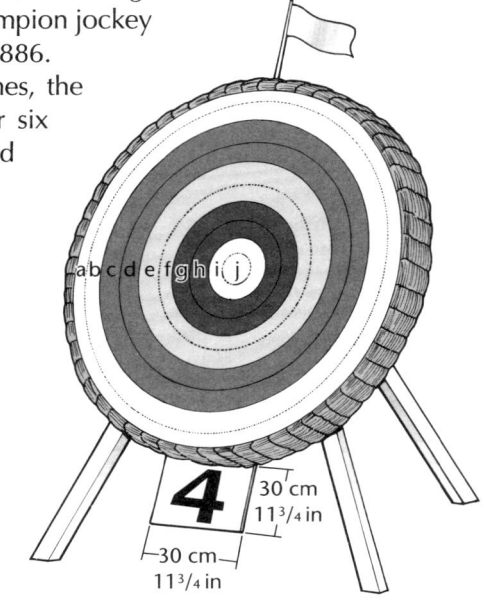

archery *3 FITA international 122 cm target face:*

a white (outer) 1 point
b white (inner) 2 point
c black (outer) 3 point
d black (inner) 4 point
e blue (outer) 5 point
f blue (inner) 6 point
g red (outer) 7 point
h red (inner) 8 point
i gold (outer) 9 point
j gold (inner) 10 point

ARCHERY IN THE UK

History
The English archers distinguished themselves in the French wars of the later Middle Ages; to this day the Queen's bodyguard in Scotland is known as the Royal Company of Archers. Up to the time of Charles II the practice of archery was fostered and encouraged by English rulers. Henry VIII in particular loved the sport and rewarded the scholar Roger Ascham for his archery treatise *Toxophilus*. In the north of England shooting for the Scorton Arrow has been carried on, with few breaks, from 1673.

Organizations
Organizations include the British Grand National Archery Society (1861), the National Archery Association (1879), US, and, for actual hunting with the bow, the National Field Archery Association (1940).

Arsenal FC

Starting life as a works football team at the Woolwich Arsenal, 'the Gunners' is one of the great British soccer clubs. They first played as Dial Square (one of the workshops within the arsenal) and then changed to Royal Arsenal. Borrowing

archery *An archer takes aim.*

red shirts (from Nottingham Forest), the works team's name evolved to Woolwich Arsenal and finally Arsenal in 1913. A series of great managers – Herbert Chapman, Bertie Mee, George Graham, and Arsene Wenger – have brought the club many honours (with Graham winning six trophies in eight years). Arsenal have been league champions 11 times and have won the **FA Cup** seven times. They have also won the League Cup (twice), the **UEFA Cup**, and the

European Cup Winners' Cup. Its women's team has won three league titles and the FA Cup three times.

Ascot
Racecourse in Berkshire, England, where The Royal Ascot race meeting, established by Queen Anne in 1711, is held annually in June. Famous for being a social as well as a sporting event, Royal Ascot is a showcase for fashion and extravagant hats, particularly on Ladies Day. Principal races include the Gold Cup, Ascot Stakes, Coventry Stakes, and the King George VI and Queen Elizabeth Stakes.

Ashes, the
Cricket trophy notionally 'held' by the winning team in the England–Australia test series. (The trophy is permanently held at **Lord's** cricket ground no matter who wins the series.) It is an urn containing the ashes of stumps and bails used in a match when England toured Australia 1882–83. The urn was given to the England captain Ivo Bligh by a group of Melbourne women. The action followed the appearance of an obituary notice in the *Sporting Times* the previous summer announcing the 'death' of English cricket after defeat by the Australians in the **Oval** test match.

> ❢ In affectionate remembrance of English Cricket. Which died at the Oval 29th August 1882. Deeply lamented by a large circle of Sorrowing Friends and Acquaintances. R.I.P. NB – The body will be cremated and the ashes taken to Australia. ❢
>
> Obituary, *The Sporting Times*, 1882.

athletics
The general name given to competitive track and field events consisting of running, throwing, and jumping disciplines. Running events range from **sprinting** (100 metres, 200 metres, and 400

metres) and **hurdles** to **cross-country running** and the **marathon** (26 mi 385 yd). Jumping events are the **high jump, long jump, triple jump**, and **pole vault**. Throwing events are the **javelin, discus, shot put**, and **hammer** throw. In the course of the last 20 years there has been increasing controversy over the unlawful use of **drugs**, such as anabolic steroids and growth hormones. The women's pole vault was included at the **Olympic Games** for the first time at Sydney, Australia, in 2000.

6 For me a day without a visit to the track is like a meal without wine or a day without sun. 9

Emile Zatopek, Czecholslovak runner, 1954.

backgammon

A board game for two players, often used in gambling. The board is marked out in 24 triangular points of alternating colours, 12 to each side. Throwing two dice, the players move their 15 pieces around the board to the six points that form their own 'inner table'; the first player to move all his or her pieces off the board is the winner.

badminton

A racket game similar to **lawn tennis** but played on a smaller court and with a shuttlecock (a half sphere of cork or plastic with a feather or nylon skirt) instead of a ball. The object of the game is to prevent the opponent from being able to return the shuttlecock. Badminton is played by two or four players. The court measures 6.1 m/20 ft by 13.4 m/44 ft. A net, 0.8 m/2.5 ft deep, is stretched across the middle of the court and at a height of 1.52 m/5 ft above the ground to the top of the net. The shuttlecock must be volleyed. Only the server can win points. The sport is named after Badminton House, the seat of the Duke of Beaufort, where the game was played in the 19th century. Major tournaments include the Thomas Cup, an international team championship for men, first held in 1949, and the Uber Cup, a women's international team competition, first held in 1957.

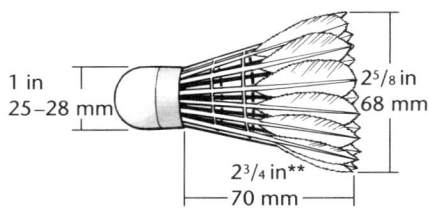

badminton *The shuttle is generally made of 16 feathers fixed in a cork base, but a combination of natural and synthetic materials or an all synthetic material are ideal in shuttles in other than top class play. The weight is 4.74–5.50 g; which determines the speed.*

ballooning

Sport or pastime of flying in an unpowered balloon. The balloons are filled with gas lighter than the surrounding air – usually hydrogen, helium, or hot air. A basket, or gondola, is attached for carrying passengers and/or instruments. In 1783, the first successful human ascent was in Paris, in a hot-air balloon designed by the Montgolfier brothers Joseph Michel and Jacques Etienne. In 1785, a hydrogen-filled balloon designed by French physicist Jacques Charles travelled across the English Channel. The first transatlantic crossing by balloon was made 11–17 August 1978 by a US team. British balloon pilot, Brian Jones, made history on 20 March 1999 when he successfully navigated his Breitling Orbiter 3 balloon on a 26,000-mile non-stop circumnavigation of the world.

❝ Flying in a balloon is so totally irrelevant and beautiful. You don't know where you're going until you get there. ❞

Bob Waligunda, balloonist, 1973.

bando or bandy

A game similar to **shinty** or **hurling**. Glamorgan coalminers used picks and shovel handles to propel the ball, and the sport's name derived from the Teutonic word 'bandja' meaning 'a curved stick'. The Bandy World Championships have been held every two years since 1957 with Russia and Sweden dominating. Although it originated in the British Isles in the late 18th century, it is now mostly played in Scandinavia, Switzerland, China, Japan, Mongolia, Germany, and the Czech Republic.

Bannister, Roger Gilbert (1929–)

English track and field athlete. He was the first person to run a mile in under four minutes. He achieved this feat at Oxford, England, on 6 May 1954, in a time of 3 min 59.4 sec.

Barcelona FC

Barcelona FC was founded in 1894. Fifteen times the winners of the Spanish championship, Barca, as it is often known, has won 24 Spanish Cup titles, the **UEFA Cup** (four times), Cup Winners' Cup (four times), European Super Cup (twice), Spanish Super Cup (five times), and Spanish League Cup (twice). Great Barca players have included Johan Cruyff, **Gary Lineker**, and **Ronaldo**.

baseball

National summer game of the USA, derived in the 19th century from the English game of **rounders**. Baseball is a bat-and-ball game played between two teams, each of nine players, on a pitch ('field') marked out in the form of a diamond, with a base at each corner. The ball is struck with a cylindrical bat, and the players try to score ('make a run') by circuiting the bases. A 'home run' is a circuit on one hit. Each year, the winner of the American League plays the winner of the National League in the **World Series**.

baseball, history of

A game called 'base ball' was played in the USA and England before 1839, founded on the old English game of **rounders**. However, baseball as we know it was first played at the Elysian Fields, Hoboken, New Jersey, in June 1846, between the Knickerbockers and the New York Nine. The National Association of Baseball Players was formed in 1858. The Cincinnati Red Stockings (now called **Cincinnati Reds**) was the first all-professional team, and in 1869 they played 64 games without defeat. The standard size and weight of ball was adopted in 1872. The catcher's mask was first worn in 1875. The National League was organized in 1876. The first chest protector came into use in 1885, and the American League became a major league in 1901. Cooperstown, New York State, contains the Baseball Hall of Fame and the National Museum of Baseball.

basketball

Ball game played between two teams of five players on an indoor enclosed court. The object is, via a series of passing moves, to throw the large inflated ball through a circular hoop and net positioned at each end of the court, 3.05 m/10 ft above the ground. The first world championship for men was held in 1950, and in 1953 for women. They are now held every four years. The object of the game is to score the most points by throwing the ball through the hoop, also called a basket.

6 Shooting is just like toenails. They may fall off occasionally but you know they'll always come back. 9

Charles Johnson, pro basketball player, 1977.

basketball, history of

Basketball was invented by James Naismith, a Canadian, who was a physical education instructor at what is now Springfield College (Massachusetts). The first game was played in 1891, and the first formal rules were set out in 1892. It rapidly became popular, especially in the eastern USA, and the first college and professional games were played before 1900. Today, the premier professional league is the National Basketball Association (NBA), formed in 1949.

Bath FC (now called Bath Rugby)

Rugby club founded in 1865. Bath FC has a long and honourable history, but it is only over the past 20 seasons that the club has truly become a giant in the English game. Coached by Jack Rowell, the club became 'professional' in approach and preparation and attracted and developed quality players who represented England and the **British Lions**. Bath is a rugby hothouse: Rowell coached England, as did two of his successors, Clive Woodward and Andy Robinson; another successor, Brian Ashton, coached Ireland. Since rugby went 'open' in 1995 and players could be paid for playing, other clubs have closed the gap on Bath. The club is now owned by greetings card millionaire Andrew Brownsword.

Beamon, Bob (1946–)

US athlete. His leap of 8.90 m/29.20 ft in the long jump final at the 1968 **Olympic Games** in Mexico City represents one of the great achievements in the history of sport, beating the previous world record by a remarkable 55 cm/21.65 in. For many years it seemed doubtful that his record would ever be broken, but in 1991 at the World Championships in Tokyo, US athlete Mike Powell jumped 8.95 m/ 29.36 ft.

Berlin Olympics

Olympic Games held in Berlin in 1936. Adolf Hitler and the Nazi party attempted to use the occasion for propaganda purposes and to demonstrate German physical prowess.

> ❝ That business with Hitler didn't bother me. I didn't go there to shake hands with him, anyway. ❞
>
> **Jesse Owens**, star of the 1936 'Nazi' Olympics, on Hitler's refusal to shake his – a black man's – hand.

Best, George (1946–)

Northern Irish footballer. One of **football's** greatest talents, he was a vital member of the great **Manchester United** side which won the league championship in 1965 and 1967, and the **European Cup** in 1968, when he was voted both English and European footballer of the year. A goal provider as much as a goal scorer, he scored 134 goals in his 349 appearances for the club 1963–73. He made 37 appearances for the Northern Ireland national team.

> ❝ I'm better than Joe Namath in both sports he participates in. I'm better than Pelé – I can kick with both feet. ❞
>
> **George Best**, 1976.

betting

Wagering money on the outcome of a game, race, or other event, not necessarily a sporting event. In the UK, on-course betting on horses and dogs may be through individual bookmakers at given odds, or on the tote (totalizator), when the total amount (with fixed deductions) staked is divided among those making the correct forecast. Off-course betting is mainly through betting 'shops' (legalized in 1960) which, like bookmakers, must have a licence. In France, there are no individual bookmakers; all betting is through the *Parimutuel*, the equivalent of the British totalizator.

biathlon

Athletic competition that combines cross-country skiing with rifle marksmanship. Basic equipment consists of cross-country skis, poles, boots, and bolt-action (non-automatic) rifles. It involves accurate shooting with rifles at prepared targets at set intervals, and is used as a military training exercise in some countries.

billiards

Indoor game played, normally by two players, with tapered poles (cues) and composition balls (one red, two white) on a rectangular table covered with a green, felt-like cloth (baize). The table has six pockets, one at each corner and one in each of the long sides at the middle. Scoring strokes are made by potting the red ball, potting the opponent's ball, or potting another ball off one of these two. In 1998 billiards received recognition from the **International Olympic Committee** as an Olympic sport, along with **snooker**, **pool**, and carom (or French) billiards. The World Professional Billiards Championship was instituted in 1870.

Black Power

The movement towards black separatism in the USA during the 1960s, embodied in the Black Panther Party, with the aim of creating a separate black state in the USA. The struggle was highlighted by protests at the Mexico Olympics in 1968, where some black athletes boycotted the games altogether while athletes John Carlos, Tommie Smith, and the relay team gave the stiff-armed black power salute when going to the podium to receive their medals. Other sports stars who supported the Black Consciousness movement included Muhammad **Ali** (who changed his name from Cassius Clay), Jim Brown (American football), and Kareem Abdul-Jabbar (basketball).

blue
A sporting term used in the UK to describe a student of Oxford or Cambridge who represents their university against the other university in a Varsity Match. This is reflected in the universities' sporting colours: Oxford wear dark blue while Cambridge play in light or 'Eton' blue. The first blues are believed to have been awarded after the 1836 **Boat Race**. Not all sports and games are automatically 'blues' sports; for example for many years, chess was a 'half-blue' sport at Cambridge but neither a blue nor half-blue sport at Oxford.

blue riband or blue ribbon
The highest distinction in any sphere. The Blue Riband of the Atlantic (Hales Trophy) is held by the vessel making the fastest crossing without refuelling. The blue riband of horse racing in the UK is held by the winner of the Derby.

BMX biking
Cross country bike racing. BMX (bicycle motocross) first became popular in the 1970s as pedal cycles were used to jump earth ramps and banks, just like unpowered motocross bikes. Arising out of the growth in popularity of BMX bikes, the first freestyle com-

---

THE THREE MAIN TYPES OF COMPETITIVE BMX EVENTS

Verts (performing grinds, flips, and spins in a half-pipe)
Dirt (which, as its name suggests, is derived from the old motocross roots of the sport)
Street (taking skills from Verts and Dirt and applying them on a track with ledges and rails).

petitions started in the 1980s. In the 1990s the sport declined relatively, but BMX bikes are still popular with teenagers, some of whom use them as an entrée to trail biking and motocross proper.

Boat Race, the

Annual UK rowing race between the crews of Oxford and Cambridge universities. It is held during the Easter vacation over a 6.8 km/4.25 mi course on the River Thames between Putney and Mortlake, southwest London. The Boat Race was first held in 1829 and there has been one dead heat in 1877. The reserve crews also have their own race. The Cambridge reserve crew is called Goldie, Oxford's is called Isis.

❝ It's Oxford! No, it's Cambridge! I can't see. It's Oxford … no … well, one of them must be winning! ❞

John Snagge, British sportscaster, 1954.

---

bobsledding or bobsleighing

The sport of racing steel-bodied, steerable toboggans, crewed by two or four people, down mountain ice-chutes at speeds of up to 80 mph/130 kph. It was introduced as an Olympic event for men in 1924, and world championships have been held every year since 1931. Women's bobsledding will be introduced to the **Olympics** at the 2002 Winter Games in Salt Lake City, Utah.

boccia

A game for disabled sportsman, boccia was first admitted to the **Paralympic Games** in 1992. Somewhat similar to bowls, with the competitors either throwing, kicking, or using a device to help propel leather balls as close as possible to a small white ball that acts as the jack (or target). The game is played indoors on a smooth flat surface, like a bowling rink, and athletes compete individually or as part of a team. Boccia is the only Paralympic sport where men and women compete together in all events.

bodybuilding

A descendent of the circus strongman tradition, bodybuilding is becoming popular as society places increasing emphasis on the 'body beautiful'. Charles Atlas was probably the first bodybuilder to achieve public acclaim, famously building up his physique so that people stopped kicking sand in his face on the beach. The emphasis on weight-training and developing a muscular body is unlike other sports, where training is a means to performing some skill faster or being stronger: here the aim is to look more physically impressive.

> 6 Many times on the beach a good looking lady will say to me, 'I want to touch you.' I always smile and say, 'I don't blame you lady.' 9
>
> **Arnold Schwarzenegger**, former Mr America and now film star, 1976.

bodybuilding, figure

A blend of bodybuilding and fitness for female competitors. The emphasis is less on pumped-up muscles than the desire to show muscle tone and body muscularity in a feminine way. Bodybuilders are judged in three rounds: the symmetry round (where competitors are judged on the equally perfect development of their bodies), a mandatory competitive round (where competitors all perform set exercises side by side, allowing judges to compare), and a free posing routine set to music.

'Bodyline'

A technique employed by **MCC** cricket captain Douglas Jardine in the 1932–33 **Ashes** series, primarily to help nullify the threat of Don **Bradman**, Australia's best player, and partly because of the LBW law as it then existed, which effectively allowed batsmen to play the ball away with their pads. The technique involved fast bowlers pitching the ball on the leg stump, forcing the batsman to play a shot. A ring of 'short-legs' fielding close to the bat waited for the mishit defensive stroke, adding to the oppressive nature of the tactic. Australia alleged the aim was to hit the batsmen, and some were badly hurt. MCC won the Ashes, but the laws were subsequently changed to prevent packed leg side fields, so making it impossible to bowl bodyline again.

bog snorkelling

Predominantly a Welsh sport, bog snorkelling involves snorkelling from one side to another of a 60-ft trench cut into a dense peat bog. The UK national championships are held each year at Llanwrtyd Wells.

Borg, Björn (1956–)

Swedish **tennis** player. He won the men's singles title at **Wimbledon** five times 1976–80, a record since the abolition of the challenge system in 1922. He also won six **French Open** singles titles 1974–75 and 1978–81 inclusive.

In 1997, at the age of 41, he played in the British leg of the ATP Seniors Tour of Europe, but lost to John **McEnroe**.

CAREER HIGHLIGHTS

Wimbledon
singles: 1976–80

French Open
singles: 1974–75, 1978–81

Davis Cup
1975 (member of winning Sweden team)

Grand Prix Masters
1980–81

WCT Champion
1976

ITF World Champion
1978–80

Botham, Ian (1955–)

English cricketer. One of the world's greatest all-rounders. In 102 Tests for England between 1977 and 1992 he scored 5,200 runs and took 383 wickets to become the first player in **Test cricket** to score over 5,000 runs as well as take over 300 wickets.

boules

French game (also called *boccie* and *pétanque*) between two players or teams; it is similar to **bowls**. Boules is derived from the ancient French game *jeu provençal*. The object is to deliver a boule (or boules) from a standing position to land as near the jack (target) as possible. The standard length of the court, normally with a sand base, is 27.5 m/90 ft.

The men's World Pétanque Championships (for teams of three) have been held annually since 1959. A women's world championship was introduced in 1988 and is held every two years.

bowling, ten pin

Indoor sport in which a ball is rolled into a target of standing pins. There are many forms of the

Botham *Ian Botham batting for England on an Australian cricket tour.*

sport, but the term 'bowling' usually refers to the most popular variety, ten pin bowling. The game is usually between two players or teams. A game of tenpins is made up of ten 'frames'. The frame is the bowler's turn to play and in each frame he or she may bowl twice. One point is scored for each pin knocked down, with bonus points for knocking all ten pins down in either one ball or two. The player or team making the greater score wins. If all ten pins go down on a first roll, it is called a 'strike' and counts as ten points plus the number of pins knocked down by the bowler's next two rolls.

bowls

Outdoor and indoor game popular in Commonwealth countries. It has been played in Britain since the 13th century and was popularized by

---

BOWLS IN THE UK

There are two popular forms of bowls played in Britain: lawn bowls, played on a flat surface, and crown green bowls, played on a rink with undulations and a crown at the centre of the green.

Francis Drake, who is reputed to have played bowls on Plymouth Hoe as the Spanish Armada approached in 1588.

The outdoor game is played on a finely cut grassed area called a rink, with biased bowls (called 'woods') 13 cm/5 in in diameter. It is played either as singles, pairs, triples, or fours. The object is to get one's bowl (or bowls) as near as possible to the jack (target).

boxing

Fighting with gloved fists. The sport dates from the 18th century, when fights were fought with bare knuckles and untimed rounds. Each round ended with a knockdown. Fighting with gloves became the accepted form in the latter part of the 19th century after the formulation of the Queensberry Rules in 1867. Contests take place in a roped ring 4.3–6.1 m/14–20 ft square. All rounds last three minutes. Amateur bouts last three rounds; professional championship bouts last as many as 12 or 15 rounds. Boxers are classified according to weight and may not fight in a division lighter than their own. The Amateur Boxing Association of England agreed in 1996 to allow women to train and fight under its rules from October 1997. At the time of the ABA decision there were no recognized professional women boxers.

Both the British Medical Association (BMA) and the American Medical Association (AMA) have repeatedly called for a ban on boxing because of the considerable risks of brain damage and disease; approximately 10% of long-term boxers develop the condition known as 'punch-drunk syndrome', which is caused by brain damage from repeated blows to the head and is characterized by slurred speech, loss of coordination, and poor memory.

❝ If I'd sat down then, I never would have gotten up. ❞

Archie Moore, world light heavyweight champion, explaining why he had refused a stool after the second round of his fight with Cassius Clay.

boxing, bare-knuckle

Bare-knuckle boxing emerged during the 18th century as a vehicle for gamblers, who bet on the outcome of the fight. Fights would continue until one boxer was unable to continue. Later, the London Prize Ring Rules gave fighters that had been knocked down 30 seconds to return to a mark scratched in the middle of the ring (the origin of the phrase 'coming up to scratch') or lose the bout. Bare-knuckle boxing was eliminated when the Queensberry Rules became the sport's rule-book, and though the practice continues in various countries, it is illegal in the UK.

boxing, history of

Boxing developed in Greece as an amateur competitive sport and was an event in the first **Olympic Games**. The Romans also boxed, with fighters often wearing studded gloves or *cesti*, which left some participants maimed or killed. But boxing declined with the Roman Empire, only to make a comeback in 18th century London when prizefighters put on bare-knuckle boxing (see **boxing, bare knuckle**) bouts as a gambling device. In 1743, the first set of prizefighting rules were drawn up by John Broughton. These governed boxing until 1838 when the London Prize Ring rules became the sport's bible. The London Prize Ring rules prevailed until they were replaced by the Queensberry Rules, drafted in 1857. For the first time, fights were fought in three-minute rounds, in defined boxing rings, and wearing boxing gloves.

Boycott, Geoffrey (1940–)

English cricketer. A prolific right-handed opening batsman for Yorkshire and England, he made 8,114 Test runs in 108 matches between 1964 and 1982 at an average of 47.72. In all first class cricket he made 48,426 runs at an average of 56.83 between 1962 and 1986. He is one of only five players to have hit over 150 first-class centuries.

Bradford City FC fire

Stadium tragedy that occured on Saturday 11 May 1985 as crowds came to Bradford City's ground at Valley Parade to celebrate as the club was proclaimed Division Three champions for 1984–85, with two games left to play. However triumph turned to tragedy as the game against Lincoln City kicked off; the main stand became engulfed in flames and 56 spectators lost their lives. It took another five years and another stadium tragedy at **Hillsborough** before the sporting authorities took action over the question of crowd safety.

Bradman, Don (1908–2001)
Australian Test cricketer. From 52 Test matches he averaged 99.94 runs per innings, the highest average in Test history. He only needed four runs from his final Test innings to average 100 but was dismissed second ball. He played for Australia for 20 years and was captain 1936–48.

Braemar
Village in Grampian, Scotland, where the most celebrated of the **Highland Games**, the Braemar Gathering, takes place on the first Saturday in September.

Breeders' Cup
End-of-season horse racing meeting in the USA, consisting of seven races. Leading horses from the USA and Europe compete for c. $10 million in prize money, the top prize going to the winner of the Breeders' Cup Classic. It was first held in 1984.

bridge
Card game derived from whist. First played among members of the Indian Civil Service about 1900, bridge was brought to England in 1903 and played at the Portland Club in 1908. It is played in two forms: **auction bridge** and **contract bridge**.

bridge, auction
A card game played by two pairs of players using all 52 cards in a standard deck. The chief characteristic is the selection of trumps by a preliminary bid or auction. It has been succeeded by **contract bridge**.

bridge, contract

Card game first played in 1925. From 1930 it quickly outgrew **auction bridge** in popularity. The game originated in 1925 on a steamer en-route from Los Angeles to Havana, and was introduced by Harold Stirling Vanderbilt (1884–1970), one of the players.

Bristow, Eric (1957–)

English darts player, nicknamed 'the Crafty Cockney'. He has won all the game's major titles, including the world professional title a record five times between 1980 and 1986.

British Lions

Rugby union side selected from the best players in the British Isles for tours of Australia, New Zealand, or South Africa. The first tour by a British side representing two or more countries took place in 1888, however the first one composed of players from all four Home Unions (England, Ireland, Scotland, and Wales) occurred in 1910. To wear the red shirt of the British Lions is considered one of the highest honours in the game.

Brooklands

Former UK motor racing track near Weybridge, Surrey. One of the world's first purpose-built circuits, it was opened in 1907 as a testing ground for early motorcars. It was the venue for the first British Grand Prix (then known as the RAC Grand Prix) in 1926. It was sold to aircraft-builders Vickers in 1946. The circuit has been rejuvenated, and now houses the Brooklands Museum.

Bruijn, Inge de (1973–)

Dutch swimmer. Specializing in the 50-metre and 100-metre freestyle and the 100-metre butterfly events, she broke three world records and tied another in her build-up to the Sydney Olympic Games in 2000. De Bruijn qualified for the 1996 Olympic Games, but decided not to go because she lost all motivation and desire to swim. De Bruijn, who finished ninth in the 100-metre butterfly event at the 1992 Olympics, said that staying home in 1996 was the biggest mistake of her life. At the Sydney Games, she won the 100-metre butterfly gold medal in 56.61 sec and in doing so lowered the world record for the third time in 2000. She also won the gold medal in both the 100-metre freestyle and 50-metre freestyle events, and contributed to a silver team medal in the 4 x 100-metre freestyle relay.

Brundage, Avery (1887–1975)
US sports administrator. He was president of the International Olympic Committee (**IOC**) 1952–72. An indomitable believer in pure amateurism, Brundage fought unyieldingly against the infiltration of commercialism into the **Olympic Games**, an inevitable tendency that accelerated greatly after his retirement.

Bruno, Frank (1961–)
English heavyweight boxer. He won the World Boxing Association (WBA) world title after defeating Oliver McCall in 1995. Bruno had made three previous unsuccessful attempts to win a world title, against Tim Witherspoon in 1986 (WBA title), Mike Tyson in 1989 (undisputed world title), and Lennox Lewis in 1993 (World Boxing Council (WBC) title). He lost his WBA title to Mike Tyson in 1996. An eye injury forced him to retire from boxing in August 1996.

Bubka, Sergey (1963–)
Ukrainian pole-vaulter who achieved the world's first six-metre vault in 1985. World champion in 1983, he was unbeaten in a

---

CAREER HIGHLIGHTS

Olympic Games	*World Champion*
champion 1988	1983, 1987, 1991, 1993, 1995, 1997
World Indoor Champion	*European Champion*
1985, 1987, 1991, 1993	1986

major event from 1981 to 1990. From 1984 he broke the world record on 32 occasions. In June 2000 he announced that he would retire after the Sydney Olympic Games in September 2000.

bullfighting

The national sport of Spain (where there are more than 400 bull-rings). It is also popular in Mexico, Portugal, and much of Latin America. It involves the ritualized taunting of a bull in a circular ring, until its eventual death at the hands of the matador. Originally popular in Greece and Rome, it was introduced into Spain by the Moors in the 11th century. Opponents of the sport criticize its cruelty, and efforts have been made to outlaw it.

Busby, Matt (1909–1994)

Scottish football player and manager, synonymous with the success of **Manchester United** both on and off the field. He was best known as manager of Manchester United 1945–69. His 'Busby Babes' won the championship in 1952, 1956, and 1957, before eight members were tragically killed in the **Munich air crash** in 1958. Busby's reassembled team reached the 1958 FA Cup final, and won the FA Cup in 1963. Championship wins in 1965 and 1967 ensured a further onslaught on European Cup competition, and the team went on to win the European Cup in 1968, the first English side to do so.

C

caber, tossing the

Scottish athletic sport, a **Highland Games** event. The caber (a tapered tree trunk about 6 m/20 ft long, weighing about 100 kg/ 220 lb) is held in the palms of cupped hands and rests on the shoulder. The thrower runs forward and tosses the caber, rotating it through 180 degrees so that it lands on its opposite end and falls forward. The best competitors toss the caber about 12 m/40 ft.

Calcutta Cup

Trophy awarded to the winner of the England v Scotland rugby union international in the **Six Nations' Championships**. The cup is a silver trophy made from Indian rupees, given to the Rugby Football Union in 1878 by the Calcutta Rugby Football Club, and has three engraved king cobras forming the handles. The Cup was damaged in 1988 after an impromptu 'soccer match' during the players' dinner; John Jeffrey (Scotland) and Dean Richards (England) were suspended following the incident.

callisthenics

A combination of gymnastics, ballet, folk dance, and music, callisthenics' roots lie in the games of ancient Greece. Its name is derived from the Greek *kallos*, meaning beauty, and *stenos*, meaning strength. **Aerobics** has developed from callisthenics, with the exercises being set to music.

camogie

Ireland's native field sport for women, a 12-a-side stick-and-ball game. It is a modified form of hurling, and the rules are very similar except that unnecessary physical contact and shouldering, or body-charging, are expressly forbidden.

Campbell, Donald Malcolm (1921–1967)

British car and speedboat enthusiast, son of Malcolm **Campbell**, who simultaneously held the land-speed and water-speed records. In 1964 he set the world water-speed record of 444.57 kph/276.3 mph on Lake Dumbleyung, Australia, with the turbojet hydroplane *Bluebird*, and achieved the land-speed record of 648.7 kph/403.1 mph at Lake Eyre salt flats, Australia. He was killed in an attempt to raise his water-speed record on Coniston Water, England.

Campbell, Malcolm (1885–1948)

British racing driver who once held both land- and water-speed records. He set the land-speed record nine times, pushing it up to 484.8 kph/301.1 mph at Bonneville Flats, Utah, USA, in 1935, and broke the water-speed record three times, the best being 228.2 kph/141.74 mph on Coniston Water, England, in 1939. His car and boat were both called *Bluebird*.

Campese, David (1962–   )

Australian rugby union player. He held the world record for the most tries scored in international rugby and is the most-capped Australian international (101 caps). **See also:** *Wallabies, the.*

canoeing

Sport of propelling a lightweight, shallow boat, pointed at both ends, by paddles or sails. Present-day canoes are made from fibreglass, but original boats were of wooden construction covered in bark or skin. Canoeing was popularized as a sport in the 19th century. Two types of canoe are used: the kayak and the Canadian-style canoe. The kayak, derived from the Inuit model, has a keel and the canoeist sits. The Canadian-style canoe has no keel and the canoeist kneels. The sport was introduced into the Olympic Games in 1936.

6 I am the only candidate who can Eskimo-roll a kayak. 9

Jimmy Carter, US presidential candidate, 1976.

Cardiff Arms Park (Welsh Parc yr Arfau)

Welsh rugby ground, officially known as the National Stadium, situated in Cardiff. The stadium became the permanent home of the Welsh national team in 1964 and has a capacity of 64,000. The stadium was demolished and replaced by the 73,000-seater **Millennium Stadium** that staged the 1999 **Rugby World Cup**. Next to the old National Stadium and new Millennium Stadium is the **Cardiff RFC** club ground, also known as Cardiff Arms Park.

Cardiff RFC

Cardiff RFC was founded in 1876 and began playing its rugby matches at Sophia Gardens before moving to **Cardiff Arms Park** where it is next door to the **Millennium Stadium**. The 'blue and blacks' won the Welsh league championship 1994–95 and 1999–2000, and the WRU Welsh Cup in 1981, 1982, 1984, 1986, 1987, 1994, and 1997. In addition, Cardiff has supplied more players for the Welsh team than any other club, though its most famous players are undoubtedly Gareth **Edwards** and Barry John, probably the greatest halfback paring ever, for club or country.

Carling, Will (William David Charles) (1965–   )

English rugby union player. A centre, he won 72 caps for England between 1988 and 1997 including a record 59 as captain. He made his full England debut in January 1988, and was appointed England captain when only 22 years old. He captained England to the Five Nations Grand Slam Championships in 1991, 1992, and 1995, the World Cup final in 1991, and the **Rugby World Cup** semi-final in 1995.

carriage driving

Sport in which two- or four-wheeled carriages are pulled by two or four horses. Events include dressage, obstacle driving, and the marathon. The Duke of Edinburgh is one of the sport's leading exponents. **See also:** *royalty and sport.*

Carson, Willie (William Fisher Hunter) (1942–   )

Scottish jockey who rode 17 English classic winners including four

Epsom Derby winners, and was the champion flat-racing jockey in 1972, 1973, 1978, 1980, and 1983. He retired in 1997 with a career total of 3,828 winners.

Cauthen, Steve (1960–   )
US jockey. He rode Affirmed to the US Triple Crown 1978 at the age of 18 and won 487 races in 1977. He twice won the English Derby, on Slip Anchor 1985 and on Reference Point 1987, and was UK champion jockey 1984, 1985, and 1987.

Celtic FC
One of the two Glasgow clubs (its great rivals are **Rangers FC**). Celtic was founded in 1888 by a Marist monk, Brother Walfrid to help raise funds for a charity for Irish immigrants to Glasgow, with the name reflecting its Scots and Irish roots. Within four years, the club had won the Scottish Cup, and the following year the league. Trophies include the European Cup, seven Premier division titles, 29 Division One titles, the Scottish Cup (31 times), the League cup (10 times), and the Glasgow Cup and Charity Cup (27 times each).

Channel swimming
A test of endurance first undertaken by Captain Matthew Webb (1848–1883) who swam across the English Channel from Dover to Calais in 1875. His time was 21 hr 45 min for the 34 km/21 mi journey. The current record is 7 hr 17 min set by Chad Hundeby of the USA in 1978. The first to swim non-stop in both directions was the Argentine Antonio Abertondo in 1961. The Channel Swimming Association was formed in 1927, and records exist for various feats; double crossing, most crossings, and youngest and oldest to complete a crossing.

Charlton, Bobby (Robert) (1937–   )
English footballer who between 1958 and 1970 scored a record 49 goals for England in 106 appearances. He spent most of his playing career with **Manchester United** and played in the England team that won the **World Cup** 1966. He was knighted in 1994.

Charlton, Jack (John) (1935–)

English footballer. He spent his playing career with Leeds United and played more than 750 games for them. He appeared in the England team that won the World Cup in 1966. He is the older brother of **Bobby Charlton**. Appointed manager of the Republic of Ireland national squad in 1986, he took the team to the 1988 European Championship finals, after which he was made an 'honorary Irishman'. He led Ireland to the **World Cup** finals for the first time in 1990 and again in 1994.

cheats, sporting

Sport has always been plagued by cheats, even in amateur days when the only prize was glory and a medal. But with the advent of professional sport and massive rewards for the winners, there is still greater pressure to be the number one. In the Olympics, sprinter Ben **Johnson** was stripped of his 100 metres crown after testing positive for drugs. The dramas of the **Tour de France** 2000 cycle race were overshadowed by drug scandals, with 45% of dope tests coming back positive, and with teams rather than individuals being accused. Cricket has been plagued by allegations of match fixing at test and one-day international level, with South African captain Hansie Cronje admitting his guilt, and other cricketers under investigation. In soccer, Anderlecht FC was banned for a year over suspicions that it tried to bribe referees.

Chelsea FC

Chelsea was formed in 1905 but did not receive its first honour until 1955, in the form of the league title. After winning the League Cup in 1965, glory came its way once more with the 1970 FA Cup, when Chelsea's hard edge saw them beat Leeds in what has been described as the dirtiest Cup Final ever. In 1971, they won the European Cup Winners' Cup, before decline set in once more. However by the end of the 1990s, Chelsea was to repeat the double, winning the **FA Cup** in 1997, the Cup Winners' Cup in 1998, and the League Cup in 1998.

Cheltenham Festival

The premier National Hunt fixture in British horse racing, known formally as the National Hunt Meeting. It has been held at Cheltenham Racecourse in Gloucestershire since 1910. The highlights of the three-day festival are the Cheltenham Gold Cup (first run 1924) and the Champion Hurdle (first run 1927).

chess

Board game originating as early as the 2nd century AD. Two players use 16 pieces each, on a board of 64 squares of alternating colour, to try to force the opponent into a position where the main piece (the king) is threatened and cannot move to another position without remaining threatened. Chess originated in India, and spread to Russia, China, Japan, and Iran. From there it was introduced to Mediterranean countries by Arab invaders. It reached Britain in the 12th century via Spain and Italy. The first official world championships were recognized in 1886.

> **CHESS PIECES**
>
> The names of chess pieces reflect the game's long history. Behind the eight pawns (foot-soldiers) on the board stand the king and queen, two bishops, two knights, and two rooks (or castles). The queen is the most powerful piece, being able to move any number of squares vertically or diagonally.

Chicago Bulls

The Bulls joined the NBA in 1967, and despite assembling tough units during its first 20 years', success has come comparatively late with the team winning six titles during the 1990s. Their success coincided with the signing of Michael **Jordan**, the most dominant player of the era and possibly the greatest ever (certainly the best-known).

Chichester, Sir Francis Charles (1901–1972)

British aviator and yachtsman who, in 1967, completed the first solo circumnavigation of the world in his yacht *Gipsy Moth IV*. The trip took 226 days. He was also the first winner of the Single-Handed Trans-Atlantic Race in 1960, completing the race in a time of 40 days, 12 hrs, 30 mins.

Cincinnati Reds

The first professional **baseball** team, Cincinnati was formed in 1869 and was a charter member of the National League. The Reds' first **World Series** win, against the Chicago White Sox in 1919, was tarnished by the discovery that the Series had been 'fixed' by gamblers and the White Sox had thrown the game. The team won four more World Series titles (and took part in four more as defeated finalists). Great players include Johnny Vander Meer and Pete Rose.

coaches and coaching

Coaches help athletes train and prepare for their sport. Some are former top class performers, while others may not have achieved great honours in the sport but are excellent communicators, technicians, and motivators. Examples of great coaches are Alex **Ferguson** (soccer), Ian McGeechan (rugby union), Tom Landry (American football), and Dan Topolski (rowing). **See also:** *Manchester United, Dallas Cowboys.*

Cobb, Ty(rus Raymond) (1886–1961)

US baseball player nicknamed 'the Georgia Peach', one of the greatest batters and base runners of all time. He played for Detroit and Philadelphia 1905–28, and won the American League batting average championship 12 times. He holds the record for runs scored (2,254) and lifetime batting average (.367). He had 4,191 hits in his career – a record that stood for almost 60 years.

Coe, Sebastian (1956–   )

English middle-distance runner, Olympic 1,500-metre champion in 1980 and 1984. He became the UK's most prolific world-record breaker with eight outdoor world records and three indoor world records (1979–81). Coe's world record for the 800 metres, set in 1981, stood for 16 years until it was broken by Wilson Kipteker of

Denmark in 1997. His 1,000-metre world record of 2 min 12.18 sec, set in 1981, was broken by Noah Ngeny of Kenya in 1999.

After his retirement from running in 1990, Coe pursued a political career with the Conservative party, and in 1992 was elected member of Parliament for Falmouth and Camborne in Cornwall. He lost his seat in the 1997 general election but has been made a life peer.

CAREER HIGHLIGHTS

Olympic Games
gold 1,500 metres 1980; silver 800 metres 1980; gold 1,500 metres 1984; silver 800 metres 1984

world records
800 metres 1979, 1981; 1,000 metres 1980, 1981; one mile: 1979, 1981 (twice); 1,500 metres 1979; 4 x 800-metre relay: 1982

Comaneci, Nadia (1961–)

Romanian gymnast. She won three gold medals at the 1976 Olympics at the age of 14, and was the first gymnast to record a perfect score of 10 in international competition. Upon retirement she became a coach of the Romanian team, but defected to Canada in 1989.

Commonwealth Games

Multisport gathering of competitors from British Commonwealth countries, held every four years. The first meeting (known as the British Empire Games) was in Hamilton, Canada, in August 1930.

Cooper, Henry (1934–)

English heavyweight boxer, the only man to win three Lonsdale Belts outright (1961, 1965, and 1970). He held the British heavyweight title 1959–1971, losing it to Joe Bugner. He fought for the world heavyweight title but lost in the sixth round to Muhammad **Ali** in 1966. He received a knighthood in the New Year's Honours list of 2000.

coxswain or 'cox'

Non-rowing member of a rowing crew, responsible for steering the boat and determining course, tactics, rowing speed etc. 'Eights' (boats with eight rowers) have a cox, while 'fours' and 'pairs' (with four and two rowers respectively) can be either 'coxed' or 'coxless'.

Cram, Steve (Stephen) (1960–)

English middle distance runner who won the 1,500 metres at the inaugural world championships in 1983, and between 1982 and 1990 also won two European and two Commonwealth gold medals and an Olympic silver medal at the same distance. In 1985, within the space of 19 days he broke world records in the mile, 1,500 metres and 2,000 metres, with times of 3 min 46.32 sec, 3 min 29.67 sec, and 4 min 51.39 sec respectively.

cricket

Bat-and-ball game between two teams of 11 players each. It is played with a small solid ball and long flat-sided wooden bats, on a round or oval field, at the centre of which is a finely mown pitch, 20 m/22 yd long. At each end of the pitch is a wicket made up of three upright wooden sticks (stumps), surmounted by two smaller sticks (bails). The object of the game is to score more runs than the opposing team. A run is normally scored by the batsman striking the ball and exchanging ends with his or her partner until the ball is returned by a fielder, or by hitting the ball to the boundary line for an automatic four or six runs.

'What is human life but a game of cricket? **9**

The Duke of Dorset, 1777.

cricket, rules

A batsman stands at each wicket and is bowled a stipulated number of balls (usually six), after which another bowler bowls from the other wicket. A batsman is usually 'out' by being either bowled out (when the ball hits the wickets and knocks off the bails), caught out, run out, stumped, or lbw (leg before wicket) – when the batsman's leg obstructs the wicket and is struck by the ball. A good captain will position fielders according to the strength of the opposition's batsman. Games comprise one or two innings, or turns at batting, per team. Two umpires arbitrate; one stands behind the wicket at the non-striker's end and makes decisions on lbw, close catches, and any infringements on the bowler's part; the other stands square of the wicket and is principally responsible for decisions on run-outs and stumpings. In Test matches, these officials are traditionally supplied by the host country, but recently there has been an increased call for neutral umpires.

cricket, history of

The exact origins of cricket are unknown, but it certainly dates back to the 16th century. The name is thought to have originated from the Anglo-Saxon word *cricc*, meaning a shepherd's staff. The first players were the shepherds of southeast England, who used their crooks as bats and the wicket gate and movable bail of the sheep pens as a target for the bowlers. It became popular in southern England in the late 18th century. Rules were drawn up in 1774 and modified following the formation of the MCC in 1787. The game's amateur status was abolished in 1963; sponsored one-day cricket was introduced in the same year. Modern bat blades are made of willow (*salix coerulea*) with handles of compressed cane and rubber; early bats were in one piece. The early Victorian period saw the introduction of protective clothing.

cricket, county

There are 18 first-class counties in the British game, and in addition to its **one-day cricket** programme, the counties play the County Championship, a series of home and away matches against the other teams over four days. In 2000, for the first time, County cricket has been organized into two divisions of nine counties.

cricket, Test

International five day cricket, known as Test cricket, is played by a number of countries: Australia, India, New Zealand, Pakistan, England, South Africa, Sri Lanka, the West Indies, and Zimbabwe. Test matches are now played over five days, though in the early years of this century, Tests were timeless. Famous grounds besides Lord's include **the Oval**, **Old Trafford**, the Melbourne Cricket Ground, and Sydney Oval, the Wankhede Stadium in Mumba, the National Stadium in Karachi, and Bagh-I-Jinnah in Lahore, Sabina Park in Jamaica, and the Wanderers' Ground, Johannesburg).

cricket, one-day
A development in the game to make it more accessible to support-ers who cannot devote several days to watch county cricket is the spread of one-day, limited-overs competitions. With matches played in a day and the rules ensuring a winner, the one-day game is thought to be more 'viewer-friendly'. Among the domestic competi-tions are the AXA Equity and Law League (formerly Refuge Assurance League), first held in 1969 and from 1999 known as the CGU National League; the NatWest Trophy (formerly called the Gillette Cup), first held in 1963; and the Benson and Hedges Cup, first held in 1972. International cricketers contest the World Cup, first held in 1975 and contested every four years.

croquet
Outdoor game played with mallets and balls on a level hooped lawn measuring 27 m/90 ft by 18 m/60 ft. Played in France in the 16th and 17th centuries, it gained popularity in the USA and England in

> ❝ Croquet is to be distinguished from cricket and chicken croquettes, which is a culinary term. It is ten times more exciting than tiddley winks and I would be very hard put to find what is less exciting. It has been called the world's worst spectator sport. ❞
>
> **G Nigel Aspinall**, All-England croquet champion, 1973.

the 1850s. Two or more players can play, and the object is to drive the balls though the hoops (wickets) in rotation. A player's ball may be advanced or retarded by another ball. The headquarters of croquet is the Croquet Association (founded 1897), based at the Hurlingham Club, London.

curling

Game played on ice with stones; sometimes described as 'bowls on ice'. One of the national games of Scotland, it has spread to many countries. At the 1998 Winter Olympics in Nagano, Japan, curling was included as a medal event for the first time.

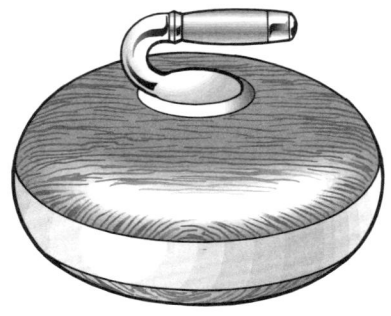

Two tees are erected about 35 m/38 yd apart. There are two teams of four players. The object of the game is to deliver the stones near the tee, those nearest scoring. Each player has two stones, of equal size, fitted with a handle. The stone is slid

curling *Stones are round, not more than 36 in/91 cm in circumference or less than 4.5 in/11.43 cm high. They must not weigh more than 44 lb/19.96 kg including the handle and boit. They are concave on the top and underneath. A boit through a centre hole screws into a goose-neck handle, which is used to deliver the stone.*

on one of its flat surfaces and it may be curled in one direction or another according to the twist given as it leaves the hand. The first world championship for men was held in 1959 and in 1979 for women.

> ❝ You should never forget that this game is played on ice – it's bound to be a little nuts. ❞
>
> **Bruce Roberts**, curling champion, 1976.

Curragh, the

Horse racing course on the Curragh Plain in County Kildare, Republic of Ireland, where all five Irish Classic races are run. It is primarily used for flat racing although it also stages races under National Hunt rules. The Curragh Plain is the national focus for horse breeding and training: the National Stud is on the edge of Kildare town, and overall some 1,300 horses are kept in the vicinity.

Curry, John Anthony (1949–1994)

English ice skater. British champion 1970 and 1972–75, and European, Olympic, and world champion 1976. He excelled in the free interpretation of music on ice, and moved the sport from the athletic to the artistic.

cycling

Riding a bicycle for sport, pleasure, or transport. Cycle racing can take place on oval artificial tracks, on the road, or across country (cyclocross and mountain biking). Among the main events are the **Tour de France**, first held in 1903; the Tour of Britain (formerly called the Milk Race), first held in 1951; and the World Professional Road Race Championship, first held at the Neuburgring, Germany, in 1927. A plan to establish a £42.5 million national cycle network in the UK was announced in 1995.

Dalglish, Kenny (Kenneth Mathieson) (1951–)

Scottish footballer and football manager. A prolific goalscorer for **Celtic** and then **Liverpool**, he was the first player to score 100 goals in both the English and Scottish first divisions. He won nine trophies as a player with Celtic and 12 with Liverpool including three European Cups. Overall, Dalglish made a record 102 international appearances for Scotland and equalled Denis Law's record of 30 goals. As a manager he won the league championship with Liverpool in 1986, 1988, and 1990, and with Blackburn Rovers in 1995.

Dallaglio, Lawrence Bruno Nero (1972–)

English rugby union player. A powerful and highly mobile flank forward, he was appointed England captain in 1997, just two years after making his full international debut. He captained **London Wasps** to their first ever English club championship 1996–97, and made a major contribution to the **British Lions** victorious tour of South Africa in 1997. In 2000 he led Wasps to victory again in the Tetley's Bitter Cup.

Dallas Cowboys

American football team formed in 1960. Known as 'America's Team', it soon became one of the most feared teams. Coached by Tom Landry until 1988, the Cowboys achieved 20 straight winning seasons, winning two **Super Bowls** during his tenure. In total the club has won five titles out of eight Super Bowls contested. Cowboy 'greats' include running back Tony Dorsett and quarterback Roger Staubach.

dancing

During the 18th century, dances such as the waltz, the polka, the mazurka, and the polonaise became popular in Britain. In the late 19th century, dances that originated in America became popular, including the mambo, cha cha cha, tango, samba, rumba, and habanera; other dances include the cakewalk, fox trot, and the Lindy or Jitterbug. The first official Ballroom Dancing World Championships were held in London in 1960, and are held every other year.

darts

Indoor game played on a circular board. Darts (like small arrow shafts) about 13 cm/5 in long are thrown at segmented targets and score points according to their landing place.

The game may have derived from target practice with broken arrow shafts in days when archery was a compulsory military exercise.

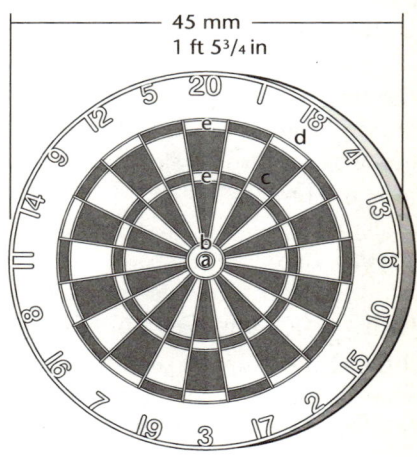

Davies, Jonathan
(1962–)
Welsh rugby union and rugby league player. He was capped 27 times between 1985 and 1988 for the Wales rugby union team. In 1988 he

darts *The dartboard is usually made of cork, bristle, or elm, with the divisions and sector numbers marked by wires. Adjacent sectors are differentiated by colour. The board is always hung so that the 20 sector is vertically above the bullseye.*

changed codes, joining **Widnes** for a fee of £225,000, and became a member of the Great Britain XIII. He was rugby league Player of the Year in 1991 and 1994. He returned to rugby union in 1995, when he joined **Cardiff**.

Davies, Laura (1963–)
English golfer. One of the longest hitters in the history of women's golf who in 1987 became the first British player to win the US Women's Open. She won the British Women's Open in 1986, and the

McDonalds LPGA Championship in 1993 and 1996, when she also won the Du Maurier Classic. In 1994 she became the first European to top the US LPGA Money List.

Davis, Joe (Joseph) (1901–1978)
British **billiards** and **snooker** player. He was world snooker champion a record 15 times 1927–46 and is responsible for much of the popularity of the game.

Davis, Steve (1957–)
English **snooker** player who has won every major honour in the game since turning professional in 1978. He has been world champion six times.

Davis Cup
Annual lawn tennis tournament for men's international teams, first held in 1900 after Dwight Filley Davis (1879–1945) donated the trophy. The Davis Cup was held on a challenge basis up to 1971. Since then it has been organized on an elimination basis, with countries divided into zonal groups, and a promotion and relegation system.

decathlon
Two-day athletic competition for men consisting of ten events: 100 metres, long jump, shot put, high jump, 400 metres (day one); 110 metres hurdles, discus, pole vault, javelin, 1,500 metres (day two). Points are awarded for performances, and the winner is the athlete with the greatest aggregate score. The decathlon is an **Olympic** event.

Derby
English horse racing event, run over 2.4 km/1.5 mi at Epsom Downs, Surrey, every June. It was established in 1780 and named after the 12th Earl of Derby. The USA has an equivalent horse race, the **Kentucky Derby**.

Desert Orchid
One of the most popular steeplechase horses in Britain. A grey gelding, he won more than 30 National Hunt races, including the King George

VI Chase in 1986, 1988, and 1989, the Cheltenham Gold Cup in 1989, and the 1990 Irish Grand National. He was ridden to most of his wins by Colin Brown, Simon Sherwood, and Richard Dunwoody.

Detroit Pistons

One of the oldest NBA franchises. The Pistons used to play at Fort Wayne until 1957, and after relocation, did not win their first NBA title until 1989 after building a team including Vinnie Johnson, Isaiah Thomas, and Kelly Tripucka. A second NBA title came in 1990. Other top Pistons include Joe Dumars, Bill Laimbeer, and Dennis Rodman.

Devers, Gail (1966–)

US athlete. In the 1990s, Devers dominated both the 100-metre sprint and 100-metre hurdles. In the 100-metre sprint she won the gold medal at the 1992 Barcelona and 1996 Atlanta Olympic Games, becoming only the second woman to win the prestigious event at two Olympics. She did not compete in 1989 and 1990 because of Graves Disease, a thyroid abnormality that caused her feet to swell so much she was within days of having them amputated. At the 1993 World Championships, she completed the sprint/hurdles double. She failed to qualify for the Sydney Olympics 2000 in the 100-metre sprint, but qualified for the hurdles though she failed to finish her semifinal heat and therefore did not make the final. Devers is best known for her dramatic fall in the 100-metre hurdles final at the 1992 Games when she fell at the last hurdle having been in contention to win the race.

DiMaggio, Joe (Joseph Paul) (1914–1999)

US baseball player with the New York Yankees 1936–51, with whom he won the World Series ten times between 1936 and 1951. In 1941 he set a record – yet to be surpassed – by getting hits in 56 con-sec-utive games. He was an outstanding fielder, played centre field, hit 361 home runs, and had a career average of .325. DiMaggio was married to the film star Marilyn Monroe between January and October 1954. He was elected to the Baseball Hall of Fame in 1955.

> 6 Joe, you never heard such cheering. 9

Marilyn Monroe, to her baseball star husband, Joe DiMaggio, on their
return to the USA from Korea.

disability sports

Sports clubs for disabled competitors have existed for over 100
years – Berlin had clubs for deaf sportsmen in 1888 – and the world
organization for sports for the deaf (CISS) was formed in 1922. It
was not until after the end of World War II that sport for physically
disabled participants was introduced, as scientists looked at exercise as a means of treating and rehabilitating servicemen's immo-
bility; the next step, to make the games competitive, followed swift-
ly. Stoke Mandeville spinal unit hosted games and the International
Stoke Mandeville Games Committee was formed in 1960; in 1964
ISOD – Internation-
al Sport Organisation
for the Disabled –
was formed, provid-
ing leadership in
sports for the blind,
amputees, cerebral
palsy sufferers, and
paraplegics. Now
the International
Paralympic Com-
mittee oversees dis-
ability sports organi-
zations worldwide.

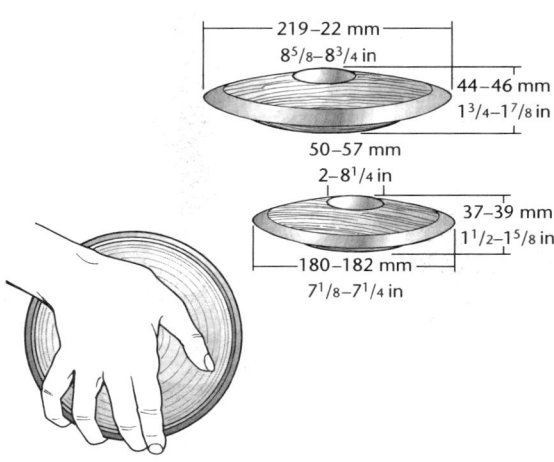

discus

Circular disc thrown
by athletes who
rotate the body to
gain momentum

discus *A smooth metal rim is permanently attached to the
body of the discus, which is made of wood or other suitable
material. A weight is secured in the centre. Minimum discus
weights are 2 kg/4 lb 6.5 oz for men, and 1 kg/2 lb 3.2 oz
for women.*
Holding the discus *The most usual method is illustrated.
Fingers must not be taped together.*

from with-in a circle 2.5 m/8 ft in diameter. The men's discus weighs 2 kg/4.4 lb and the women's 1 kg/2.2 lb. Discus throwing was a competition in ancient Greece at gymnastic contests, such as those of the **Olympic Games**. It is an event in the modern Olympics and athletics meetings.

diving

Sport of entering water either from a springboard 1 m/3 ft or 3 m/10 ft above the water, or from a platform, or highboard, 10 m/33 ft above the water.

diving *A minimum pool depth of 5 m/16.5 ft is needed for high or platform*

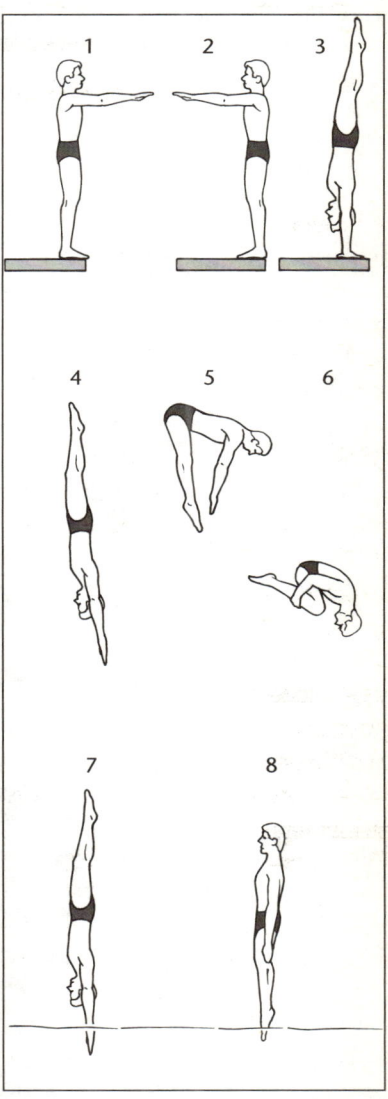

diving *The three stages of a dive are the take-off from the board, the flight (fall through the air), and the entry into the water.*

Various differing starts are adopted, facing forwards or backwards, and somersaults, twists, and combinations thereof are performed in mid-air before entering the water. A minimum pool depth of 5 m/16.5 ft is needed for high or platform diving. Points are awarded and the level of difficulty of each dive is used as a multiplying factor.

diving, cliff

A diving event, which is staged less for competition than for entertainment, cliff diving from rocky ledges or cliffs into the waters below is a spectator sport, especially in Acapulco where diners watch from the terraces. Diving from around 100 ft/30.5 m up, often into shallow water or rocky pools, the dive is very risky.

dogsled racing

The first recorded dogsled race took place in 1908 with the All Alaska Sweepstake over a 408-mile course, which was completed in a time of 119 hours, 15 mins, 12 secs. In 1910 the time was slashed to 74 hours, 14 mins, 37 secs, which is still the record to this day. Now the sport is regulated by the International Dogsled Racing Association, with member countries from all over the world including England, Australia, and Japan. **See also:** *Iditarod*.

dope testing

Competitors in a variety of sports are routinely drug tested, and those found to have taken performance enhancing drugs may be suspended or banned by their sport's governing body. Tests may be ordered randomly among competitors or may concentrate on the first three competitors. Both methods of testing may be adopted in some major athletics competitions. In addition, out-of-competition testing also increases the chances of detection. Samples are analyzed at a number of laboratories worldwide. These enjoy a high reputation for accuracy, though there has been some concern that a number of extremely high nandrolone test readings may have occurred naturally.

Dragila, Stacy (1971–   )
US athlete. At the Sydney Olympic Games 2000, Stacy Dragila completed an historic triple by winning the gold medal in the women's pole vault Olympic debut. She had also won the gold medal at the first women's pole vault event held at the World Indoor Championships in 1997, and the World Championships in 1999. In May 2000, she took the world record at the US Olympic Track and Field Trials.

dragon boat racing
Dragon boats are long, multicoloured boats of traditional Chinese design. They measure anything from 30–100 ft long and are wide enough to hold two paddlers side-by-side. Decorated with dragon's heads, long tails, and scaly bodies, rowing races involving dragon boats have evolved from a religious festival, normally held on 'the fifth of the fifth' (the fifth day of the fifth month), into an entertainment and recreation, with dragon boat races held worldwide.

drag racing
Motor sport popular in the USA. High-powered single-seater cars with large rear and small front wheels are timed over a 402.2 m/440 yd strip. Speeds of up to 530 kph/330 mph have been attained by the fastest type of drag-racing cars, 'top fuel' dragsters – the other categories of professional drag-racing vehicles are 'funny cars', 'pro-stock', and 'pro-stock bikes'.

draughts
Board game (known as checkers in the USA and Canada because of the chequered board of 64 squares) with elements of a simplified form of **chess**. Each of the two players has 12 men (disc-shaped pieces), and attempts either to capture all the opponent's men or to block their movements.

dressage
Method of training a horse to carry out a predetermined routine of specified movements. Points are awarded for discipline and style.

drugs in sport

'Doping' is the use of banned substances or methods by athletes that may enhance their performance. Drugs are banned for various reasons – ethical (they may enhance performance above natural levels), medical (prolonged drug use may harm competitors), and legal (some banned athletic substances are also banned in the wider community, like cocaine). **See also:** *dope testing.*

BANNED DRUGS AND PROCEDURES

Prohibited substances include stimulants like amphetamine, anabolic steroids, human growth hormones, and narcotic painkillers. Banned practices include blood doping, where blood is removed from the body then reintroduced shortly before competition, giving the athlete a greater oxygen capacity.

E

Edgbaston

One of Warwickshire's county cricket ground, located near Birmingham. It is one of the English Test match grounds, though its pitches have been criticized in recent years.

Edwards, Gareth Owen (1947–)

Welsh rugby union player. A fast, elusive scrum-half, he scored 20 tries in 53 internationals for Wales between 1967 and 1978. He toured with the **British Lions** three times winning a further 10 international caps. Appointed captain of Wales in 1968 at the age of only 20, he appeared in seven Five Nations championship winning teams, five Triple Crown winning teams, and three Grand Slam winning teams. **See also:** *Cardiff RFC.*

Edwards, Jonathan David (1966–)

English athlete who won the triple jump title at the 1995 World Championships in Gothenburg with a world record leap of 18.29 metres. He won a gold medal at the 2000 **Olympic Games** and a silver medal at the 1996 Games. He also won a silver medal at the 1997 World Championships, a gold at the 1998 European championships, and a bronze medal at the World Championships in Seville, Spain, in 1999.

CAREER HIGHLIGHTS

World Championship
bronze 1993, gold 1995, silver 1997, bronze 1999

Olympic Games
silver 1996, gold 2000

European Championships
gold 1998

Commonwealth Games
silver 1990, silver 1994

electronic timing (athletics)

The timing of track events used to be determined by officials sitting in the stands starting a stopwatch when the smoke from the starter's gun was visible. Today, the starting gun is electronic and as well as giving off a sound, it also activates the timing and photo finish mechanism. The photo finish is actually a slit camera that is aimed at the finishing line and records the finishing order in relation to time. This is often now video-based and records race times to 1/1,000 of a second.

equestrianism

Skill in horse riding, as practised under International Equestrian Federation rules. An Olympic sport, there are three main branches of equestrianism: showjumping, dressage, and three-day eventing. Three other disciplines are under the

The safety of three-day eventing was called into question in 1999 after an unprecedented spate of fatal accidents at British horse trials. Between May and September, four riders, including the British Olympic prospect Polly Phillipps, were killed.

THREE BRANCHES OF EQUESTRIANISM

Showjumping is horse-jumping over a course of fences. The winner is usually the competitor with fewest 'faults' (penalty marks given for knocking down or refusing fences), but in timed competitions it is the competitor completing the course most quickly, additional seconds being added for mistakes.

Dressage tests the horse's obedience skills and the rider's control. Tests consist of a series of movements at walk, trot, and canter, with each movement marked by judges who look for suppleness, balance, and a special harmony between rider and horse. The term is derived from the French 'dresser', which means training. It became an Olympic sport in 1960.

Three-Day Eventing tests the all-round abilities of a horse and rider in dressage, cross-country, and showjumping.

authority of the International Equestrian Federation (FEI): **carriage driving**, endurance riding, and vaulting.

Eton Field Game
A form of football confined to Eton public school, the Eton Field Game is an 11-a-side game that differs from soccer in the small size of the ball, the small goal, the absolute bar on handling the ball, and some other minor differences.

Eton Wall Game
One of the oldest forms of football in existence, and unique to Eton College, the Eton Wall Game is played on a pitch where an 11-ft high brick wall is adjacent to the field. Ten players on either side contest the game in a narrow strip five yards wide and 118 yards long.

European Championships (football)
First staged in 1960 and held every four years thereafter, the European Championship is contested by national teams, first in preliminary group rounds and then in a final comprising a group stage followed by a knock-out stage. The Euro 2000 event finals, held in Belgium and the Netherlands, was contested by 16 teams, with 49 teams taking part in the preliminary stages.

European Cup (athletics)
First contested in 1965 by European nations, initially on a two-year cycle but now held every year. The brainchild of former IAAF European committee president Bruno Zauli, the winning team is presented with a trophy named after him.

European Cup (rugby)
The Heineken Cup as it is called is an annual club competition between clubs from Great Britain, France, and Ireland. The first tournament was held 1996–97 and was won by Brive. Since then **Bath**, Ulster, and Northampton have also lifted the trophy. The competition is a two-stage event, with a pool stage followed by a knockout event.

Eusebio (1942–)

Adopted name of Eusebio Ferreira da Silva, Portuguese footballer, born and brought up in Mozambique (Portuguese East Africa). He made his international debut in 1961 and played for his country 64 times, scoring 41 goals. He spent most of his league career with Benfica, but also played in the USA. Between 1961 and 1973 he scored 316 goals in 294 league games for Benfica and won 10 championship winners' medals. He was European Footballer of the Year in 1965.

Evert, Chris(tine Marie) (1954–)

US **tennis** player. She won her first **Wimbledon** title in 1974, and has since won 21 Grand Slam titles. She became the first woman tennis player to win $1 million in prize money. Evert was a great exponent of baseline technique and had an outstanding two-handed backhand. From 1974 to 1989 she never failed to reach the quarter-finals at Wimbledon. Everet married British Davis Cup player John Lloyd in 1979, but subsequently divorced him. She retired from competitive tennis in 1989 and is known for her charity work; she has raised well over $7 million in nine years.

CAREER HIGHLIGHTS

Wimbledon
singles: 1974, 1976, 1981;
doubles: 1976

US Open
singles: 1975–78, 1980, 1982

French Open
singles: 1974–75, 1979–80, 1983, 1985–86; doubles: 1974–75

Australian Open
singles: 1982, 1984

❝ It would be very nice if some writer would get around to describing me as sexy. ❞

Chris Evert, tiring of the emphasis on her youth, 1972.

Everton FC

One of the Merseyside teams, Everton was founded in 1878 as St Domingo FC and became a professional side in 1885. 'The Toffees' play at Goodison Park, Liverpool, and great players include Dixie Dean and Neville Southall. In 2000, they signed Paul **Gascoigne** on a free transfer.

extreme sports

Non-traditional, non-competitive activities that demand athletic skill and a willingness to take risks. Unlike confrontational sports, there is no challenge from an opponent; instead the difficulty of the activity itself is the challenge. Examples of extreme sports are bungee jumping, BASE-jumping, extreme skiing, mountain biking, extreme free rock climbing, snowboarding, and white-water canoeing. In all extreme events, the key element is danger.

FA, the (Football Association)

The governing body of **association football** in England, initially responsible for codifying the game and unifying the different rules under which it was played (though responsibility for drawing up the laws of the game now rests with FIFA). The **FA Cup**, first held 1871–72, was football's first national tournament. The FA sponsored the creation of the football league and divisional soccer in the UK.

FA Cup (Football Association Challenge Cup)

The major annual **soccer** knockout competition in England and Wales, open to all member clubs of the English **FA**. First held 1871–72, it is the oldest football knockout competition.

FAI, the (Football Association of Ireland)

Association football was first introduced to Ireland in 1878, and the FAI formed in 1880. The country's first club, Cliftonville, had been formed in 1879 and Ireland's first international side took to the field in 1881, losing 13–0 to England. As well as

FA Cup *The FA Cup trophy.*

administering the game in Ireland and running the national side, the FAI is planning a new stadium at Citywest, west Dublin.

Faldo, Nick (Nicholas Alexander) (1957–)

English golfer who was the first Briton in 54 years to win three British **Open** titles, and the only person after Jack Nicklaus to win two successive US **Masters** titles (1989 and 1990). He is one of only seven golfers to win the Masters and British Open in the same year.

Fangio, Juan Manuel (1911–1995)

Argentine racing-car driver who won the drivers' world championship a record five times 1951–57. For most of his career he drove a blue and yellow Maserati.

Fed Cup

International tennis tournament for women's teams first held in 1963 (then called the Federation Cup) and similar to the men's **Davis Cup** competition although with some differences in format. The competition was renamed the Fed Cup in 1995.

fencing

Sport of fighting with swords including the **foil**, derived from the light weapon used in practice duels; the **épée**, a heavier weapon derived from the duelling sword proper; and the **sabre**, with a

fencing *A display fight in Berlin in 1920 between the then European champion of foil fencing, Politi, and Helene Mayer.*

curved handle and narrow V-shaped blade. In sabre fighting, cuts count as well as thrusts. Masks and protective jackets are worn, and hits are registered electronically in competitions. Men's fencing has been part of every Olympic programme since 1896; women's fencing was included from 1924 but only using the foil.

Fencing

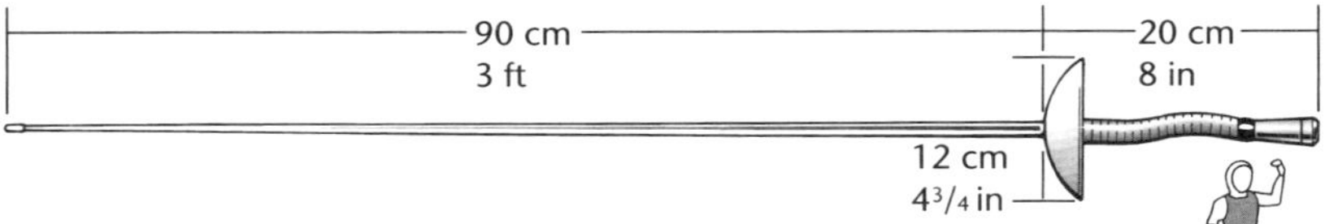

├─────────── 90 cm ───────────┤   ├── 20 cm ──┤
              3 ft   8 in

12 cm
4³/₄ in

target
area

Foil: introduced in the 17th century; a thin, flexible blade with a rectangular cross section and small guard to protect the hand. Body target is the torso.

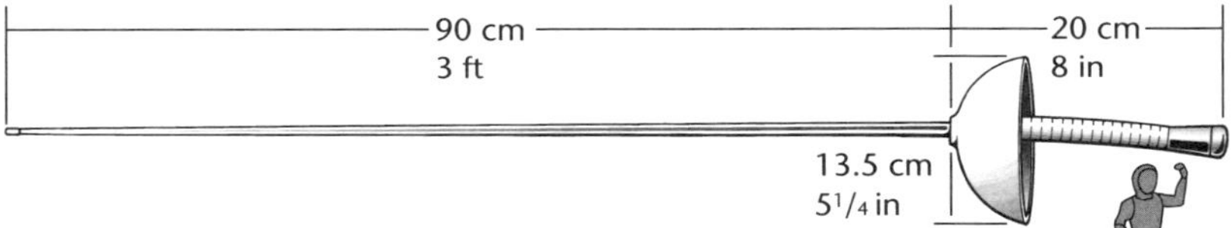

├─────────── 90 cm ───────────┤   ├── 20 cm ──┤
              3 ft   8 in

13.5 cm
5¹/₄ in

Épée: introduced in the 17th century; a thin, flexible blade with a rectangular cross section and small guard to protect the hand. The entire body is the target.

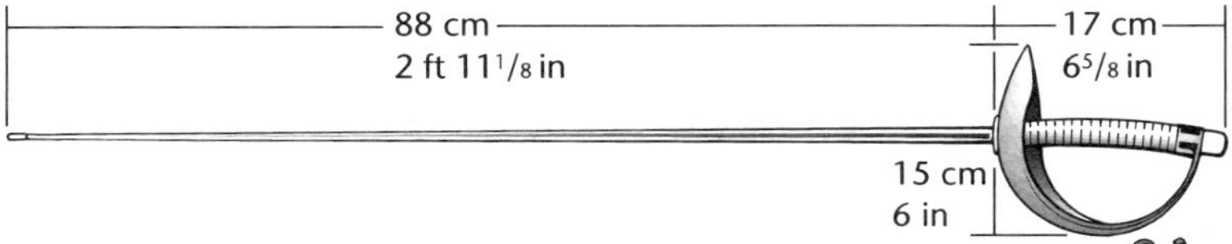

├─────────── 88 cm ───────────┤   ├── 17 cm ──┤
         2 ft 11¹/₈ in   6⁵/₈ in

15 cm
6 in

Sabre: introduced in the late 19th century; a light flat blade with a knuckle guard which completely covers the hand. The whole body above the waist is the target.

Ferguson, Alex(ander) (1941–)

Scottish football manager. One of British football's most successful managers. Since 1986 he has won 14 trophies with **Manchester United** including six league championship titles and four FA Cups. In 1999, under his charge, Manchester United became the first club to achieve the league championship and **FA Cup** double three times, having previously performed the feat in 1994 and 1996. Also in 1999 he led Manchester United to the European Cup, thus achieving a unique treble in English football. Earlier, as manager of

Aberdeen from 1978 to 1986, he won 10 trophies including three Scottish championships and the European Cup Winners' Cup. He was manager of the Scottish national side 1985–86. He was knighted in 1999.

field sports
Traditional country pursuits of hunting, shooting, and fishing. They are regulated both by law and social custom. Increasing public concern has been expressed about the suffering they may cause to animals, particularly in the case of fox-hunting. The term 'field sports' refers only to selected activities. Hunting is the pursuit of quarry with hounds, for example fox hunting, deerhunting, and beagling (hunting hares on foot). In coursing, hares are pursued by greyhounds or lurchers as a test of the dogs' skill. In fishing the term is confined to the catching of trout and salmon using artificial flies. Shooting is a highly organized activity in which pheasants, partridges, or grouse are specially reared and later released as targets.

Fischer, Bobby (Robert James) (1943–)
World Chess Champion 1972–75 and 1992. In 1958, after proving himself in international competition, he became the youngest grand master in history. He was the author of *Games of Chess* (1959), and was also celebrated for his unorthodox psychological tactics. **See also:** *chess.*

❝I like to see my opponents squirm.❞

Bobby Fischer, 1972.

fishing or angling
Fishing with a rod and line. It is widespread and ancient in origin, fish hooks having been found in prehistoric cave dwellings. Competition angling exists and world championships take place for most branches of the sport. The oldest is the World Freshwater

Championship, inaugurated in 1957. Angling is the largest partici-
pant sport in the UK.

TYPES OF FISHING

Freshwater fishing embraces coarse fishing, in which members of the
carp family, pike, perch, and eels are taken by baits or lures; and game
fishing, in which members of the salmon family, such as salmon and
trout, are taken by spinners (revolving lures) and flies (imitations of adult
or larval insects).

In *sea fishing* the catch includes flatfish, bass, and mackerel; big-game
fishes include shark, tuna (or tunny), marlin, and swordfish.

❝ When you're out there and see 50 tarpon coming at
you with their mouths open, well, the thrill of it just
sort of makes your knees go wobbly. ❞

Gene Montgomery, Florida fishing guide.

fives

Game of handball, where two or four players hit a hard ball against
a wall or walls with padded gloves. In England there are three forms
of the game, distinguished from one another by the names of the
schools in which they were variously played: Eton, Rugby, and
Winchester Fives. Under the name of handball a similar game is
played in the USA and Ireland.

footbag or hackey sack

A competitive sport since the 1970s, footbag net is a singles or doubles court game, like tennis or volleyball, where players use their
feet to kick the footbag over a 5 ft/1.52 m net on a court measuring
20 ft x 44 ft/6.10 m x 13.41 m, divided into four quadrants, with
games played to 11 or 15 points where players need to win by two

points. In addition, footbag freestyle is a more artistic form of the sport, more akin to dancing or skating, where players perform difficult manoeuvres and routines to music.

football, American

Contact sport similar to the English game of **rugby**, played between two teams of 11 players, with an inflated oval ball. The **Super Bowl**, first held in 1967, is now an annual meeting between the winners of the National and American Football Conferences.

The game is played on a field marked out with a series of regularly spaced parallel lines giving a gridiron effect. There is a goalpost at each end of the field, and beyond this an end zone. Games are divided into four quarters of 15 minutes each. Points are scored by running or passing the ball across the goal line (touchdown, 6 points); by kicking it over the goal's crossbar after a touchdown (conversion, 2 points), or from the field during regular play (field goal, 3 points); or by tackling a defending player who has the ball in the end zone, or blocking a defending team's kick so it goes out of bounds from the end zone (safety, 2 points). A team consists of more than 40 players but only 11 are allowed on the field at any one time.

football, American, equipment

American football is a full contact sport; players make hits on their opposition whether they are in possession of the ball or not. To protect themselves the players wear elaborate equipment, including lightweight plastic padding covering thighs, hips, shoulders, knees, and sometimes forearms and hands (the type of padding differs depending on the player's position: for example kickers who are only on the field for short periods of time tend to wear less padding). Players also wear plastic helmets with guards that protect most of the facial area.

football, American, history of

The first game of football is generally accepted as having been played between Rutgers and Princeton universities in November 1869, when teams of 25 players took to the field (though this was reduced to 20 players in 1873, 15 in 1876, and 11 in 1880). College football was very popular throughout the 20th century, with the universities producing many of the great stars of the professional game, especially after World War II when sporting scholarships allowed many fine athletes to take advantage of a college education by trading on their sporting prowess. The first professional football game was played in 1895 at Latrobe, Pennsylvania. Over the next few decades more professional teams were formed, with college players being recruited into the pro game. The first league, the American Professional Football Association, was set up in 1920, in 1922 the National Football League was created, though at this stage players, though paid, were part-timers, often with other jobs, and not the full-time professionals of today.

football, Association (soccer)

Form of football originating in the UK and popular throughout the world. The modern game is played in the UK according to the rules laid down by the home countries' football associations. Slight amendments to the rules take effect in certain competitions and international matches as laid down by the sport's world governing body, Fédération Internationale de Football Association (FIFA, 1904). FIFA organizes the competitions for the **World Cup**, held every four years since 1930. The field has a halfway line marked with a centre circle, two penalty areas, and two goal areas. The game is played with an inflated spherical ball. There are two teams each of 11 players, broadly divided into defence (the goalkeeper and defenders), midfield (whose players collect the ball from the defence and distribute it to the attackers), and attack (forwards or strikers). The object of the game is to kick or head the ball into the opponents' goal. It is played for two periods of 45 minutes each, the teams changing ends at half time.

football, Association, history of

The modern game began in the 19th century, when a variety of schools and universities played ball games allowing both kicking and handling of the ball. The first laws were drafted in 1862, and in 1863 the sport was split into rugby football and association football (which banned the use of the hands). Once the **FA Cup** was instituted, the game spread rapidly, leading to the acceptance of professionalism in 1885 and

football *A 19th-century illustration of a football game.*

regular league soccer in 1888. The British Empire helped spread the game across the globe, with sailors and colonialists taking the game to the colonies where French, German, Italian, and Austrian colonialists adopted the game. FIFA was formed in 1904 and in 1930 the first **World Cup** was held. Most countries now hold domestic cup competitions and leagues, with the incentives of promotion and the chance to play in European or other international club competitions. The USA resisted soccer's charms as a men's sport for most of the 20th century, though it is now the fastest-growing school and college sport. US women have embraced it wholeheartedly, and the USA is the holders of the Women's World Cup.

football, Australian Rules or Australian football or Australian national football

An 18-a-side game that originated on the goldfields of Victoria in the 1850s. It is an adaptation of the Gaelic football played by Irish miners. This code is the major form of football played in Victoria, South Australia, Western Australia, and Tasmania. The largest attendances are in Victoria where the Victorian Football League (VFL) was formed in 1897. It was renamed the Australian Football League (AFL) in 1989.

football, Gaelic

Kicking and catching game played mainly in Ireland. The two teams have 15 players each. The game is played on a field with an inflated spherical ball. The goalposts have a crossbar and a net across the lower half. Goals are scored by kicking the ball into the net (three points) or over the crossbar (one point). First played in 1712, it is now one of the sports under the auspices of the **Gaelic Athletic Association**. The leading tournament is the All-Ireland Championship (first held in 1887); its final is played in Dublin on the third Sunday in September each year, the winners receiving the Sam Maguire Trophy.

Foreman, George (1948–   )

US heavyweight boxer who was the undisputed world heavyweight champion 1973–74. He turned professional after winning the heavyweight gold medal at the 1968 Olympic Games. Foreman had retired from boxing in 1977, but returned to the sport in 1987. In November 1994, at the age of 45, Foreman became the oldest world heavyweight champion when he knocked out Michael Moorer to win the International Boxing Federation (IBF) and World Boxing Association (WBA) heavyweight title belts. He was stripped of his WBA title in 1995 and his IBF title a year later, in both cases refusing to fight the official challenger. He retired in 1997, 28 years after making his professional debut. In total, he won 76 of his 81 professional fights, knocking out or stopping his opponents in 68 of them.

Formula 1

Formula 1 (F1) is the fastest, most sophisticated level of single seat racing cars that compete under the auspices of FIA, the car racing governing body. Other classes of formula cars (in descending order) are Formula 2, Formula 3, Formula Atlantic, Formula Renault, and Formula Ford.

Fosbury, Dick (1947–   )

US track and field athlete. He revolutionized the high jump with his back-first 'Fosbury Flop', and won a gold medal in the event at the 1968 **Olympic Games**.

Freeman, Cathy (1973–   )
Australian track athlete. At the Sydney **Olympic Games** 2000 she represented Australia and her Aboriginal heritage by lighting the Olympic flame in the opening ceremony, and at the Games went on to win the gold medal in the 400 metres, an event in which she was the clear favourite having won the previous two World Championships. Freeman is extremely proud of her heritage. At the 1994 Commonwealth Games, she took her victory lap wrapped in the Aboriginal flag before taking a second lap with the Australian flag. She repeated this act again following her 400-metre victory at the 1997 World Championships. For her cultural and athletic accomplishments, she was named the 1998 Australian of the Year, one of the country's highest civilian honours.

Gaelic Athletic Association (GAA)

Irish association founded in November 1884 in Tipperary by the Irish sportsmen Micheal Cusack and Maurice Davin. Its aims were to promote and develop traditional Irish pastimes, namely **hurling** and **Gaelic football**. After rules were drawn up for the games, the first All-Ireland finals were held three years later. Initially it was very wary of outside influences, and introduced a controversial 'ban' which threatened expulsion to any member involved in foreign sports such as soccer and rugby. Although the ban was not universally approved of, it remained in place for almost a hundred years. The games themselves thrived, and hurling and football are Ireland's two most popular sports today.

gambling or gaming

Staking of money or anything else of value on the outcome of a competition. Forms of gambling include betting on sports results, casino games like blackjack and roulette, card games like poker, slot machines, and lotteries. Association football (via football pools) and horse racing attract gambling through either off- or on-course betting.

In the UK commercial gambling is restricted to premises licensed and registered under statute.

> ❝ It is strange to see people of this poor rank, that look as if they had not bread to put in their mouth, still bet and lose it. ❞
>
> **Samuel Pepys**, diarist, 1663, after watching his first cockfight.

Gascoigne, Paul (1967–)

Nicknamed Gazza, English footballer who played for Newcastle United 1985–87, **Tottenham Hotspur** 1988–91, Lazio, Italy 1992–95, **Rangers** 1995–97, and then Middlesbrough. He made his full England debut in September 1988 and by August 1998 he had won 57 caps. He became a national hero after the 1990 **World Cup** finals in Italy, as much for his tearful response to receiving a booking in the semi-final against West Germany (which would have ruled him out of the final had England won the match) as for his brilliant performances in England's midfield.

gliding

The art of using air currents to fly unpowered aircraft. Technically, gliding involves the gradual loss of altitude; gliders designed for soaring flight (utilizing air rising up a cliff face or hill, warm air rising as a thermal above sun-heated ground, and so on) are known as sailplanes. Gliding played an important part in the development of flight. Pioneers include George Cayley, Otto Lilienthal, Octave Chanute (1832–1910), and the Wright brothers, the last-named perfecting gliding technique in 1902. Because of the ban on military flying, gliding made great progress in Germany between the two world wars. In World War II, towed gliders were used by the Germans in Crete and the Allies at Arnhem, the Netherlands, to provide additional carrying capacity for troops and equipment. These transport gliders were expendable and could be landed in open country away from airfields, and the troops required no special training such as is necessary for parachutists.

go

Board game originating in China 3,000 years ago, and now the national game of Japan. It is played by placing small counters on a large grid. The object is to win territory and eventual superiority. The board, squared off by 19 horizontal and 19 vertical lines, begins empty and gradually fills up with black and white counters (originally flattish, rounded stones) as the players win territory by surrounding areas of the board with 'men' and capturing the enemy armies by surrounding them. A handicapping system enables expert and novice to play against each other.

goalball
A team sport for two teams of three visually impaired players. All players are blindfolded to allow sighted, partially sighted, and blind competitors to play together. The object of the game is to roll a ball (which weighs 1.25 kg/2.76 lb and contains noise bells) across the opposing team's goal line using a bowling action. (Only blind competitors can play in international teams.)

golf
Outdoor game in which a small rubber-cored ball is hit with a wooden- or iron-faced club into a series of holes using the least number of shots. On the first shot for each hole, the ball is hit from a tee, which elevates the ball slightly off the ground; subsequent strokes are played off the ground. Most courses have 18 holes and are approximately 5,500 m/ 6,000 yd in length. Golf developed in Scotland in the 15th century.

Each hole is made up of distinct areas: the *tee*, from where players start at each hole; the *green*, a finely manicured area where the hole is located; the *fairway*, the grassed area between the tee and the green, not cut as finely as the green; and the *rough*, the perimeter of the fairway, which is left to grow naturally. Natural hazards such as trees, bushes, and streams make play more difficult, and there are additional hazards in the form of sand-filled bunkers and artificial lakes.

❝ What is there in life but golf and girls? ❞

Jim Colbert, US pro golfer, 1977.

golf clubs
Clubs consist of *woods* and *irons*, and are numbered according to the angle at which the face of the club is set (the higher the number, the more acute the angle; clubs with a straight face send the ball the

furthest). Most players also carry a wedge, a faced iron set at a sharp acute angle with a deep flange, this being ideal for bunker play. All carry a putter for holing out on the greens; this is the only club that has a wide variety of shapes to suit individual styles.

golf, history of

The name 'golf' is almost certainly derived from the German *kolbe*, meaning club. It was also called *goff* and in vulgar Scots *gowff*. Games of club and ball were common to all countries, and at their simplest consisted of trying to hit a ball furthest with a single stroke (as in the very early version

golf *A 19th century engraving of the famous St Andrews golf course in Scotland.*

of the French game *pall-mall*). The next development was to try to cover a much longer distance in the fewest possible strokes (as in the Flemish game *chole*). Another variant was a test of accuracy, the ball having to strike a mark (as in the Dutch game *kolven*). It was, however, the Scottish game that became the basis of modern golf, combining distance-hitting with the test of aiming the ball into a hole, and the essential idea of the independent progress of the contestants, each playing free from any interference by their opponent. The first properly constituted clubs were the Honourable Company of Edinburgh Golfers 1744, the Royal and Ancient Golf Club of St Andrews 1754, the Royal Blackheath Golf Club 1766, and the Royal Musselburgh Golf Club 1774.

Goodwood

Racecourse northeast of Chichester, West Sussex, England, founded in 1802 by the third Duke of Richmond. Its races include the Goodwood Cup and Sussex Stakes, held in July/August. A motor-racing track used between 1948 and 1966 was reopened in 1998 for historic racing, and since 1993 Goodwood has hosted the Festival of Speed, an annual celebration of classic motor-racing.

Grace, W(illiam) G(ilbert) (1848–1915)

English cricketer. By profession a doctor, he became the most famous sportsman in Victorian England. A right-handed batsman, he began playing first-class cricket at the age of 16, scored 152 runs in his first Test match, and scored the first triple century in 1876. Throughout his career, which lasted nearly 45 years, he scored 54,896 runs and took 2,876 wickets.

He scored 2,739 runs in 1871, the first time any batsman had scored 2,000 runs in a season. An all-rounder, he took nearly 3,000 first-class wickets. Grace played in 22 Test matches.

CAREER HIGHLIGHTS

All first-class cricket
runs: 54,896; average: 39.55; best: 344 (MCC v Kent, 1876)
wickets: 2,876; average: 17.92; best: 10–49 (MCC v Oxford University, 1886)

Test cricket
runs: 1,098; average: 32.29; best: 170 (v Australia, 1886)
wickets: 9; average: 22.26; best: 2–12 (v Australia, 1890)

Grand National

Horse-race held in March or April at **Aintree**, Liverpool, England. The most famous steeplechase race in the world, it was inaugurated in 1839 as the Grand Liverpool Steeple Chase, adopting its present name in 1847.

Grand National *Racehorses Three Brownies (nearest the camera) and Sure Metal jump The Chair, the highest jump of the Grand National at 5 ft 2 in/1.56 m high.*

The current course is 7.24 km/ 4.5 mi long, with 30 formidable jumps. The highest jump is the Chair at 156 cm/5 ft 2in. Grand National steeplechases based on the Aintree race are held in Scotland, Wales, and Ireland at Ayr, Chepstow, and Fairyhouse respectively.

grand slam

In tennis, the winning of four major tournaments in one season: the **Australian Open**, the **French Open**, **Wimbledon**, and the **US Open**. In golf, it is also winning the four major tournaments in one season: the **US Open**, the British **Open**, **the Masters**, and the **PGA** (Professional Golfers Association) National Championship. In **baseball**, a grand slam is a home run with runners on all the bases. A grand slam in bridge is when all 13 tricks are won by one team.

Grey, Tanni (1969–   )

British athlete. She won gold medals in the 100, 200, 400, and 800 metres wheelchair races at both the 1992 **Paralympic Games** at Barcelona and the 1994 world championships at Berlin. She won the women's wheelchair event at the London Marathon in 1992, 1994, 1996, and 1998. Also in 1998, she won gold in the 800 metres wheelchair event at the European Championships in Budapest, Hungary.

greyhound racing

Spectator sport, invented in the USA in 1919, in which a number of greyhounds pursue a mechanical hare around a circular or oval track. It is popular in Great Britain and Australia, attracting much on- and off-course betting. The leading race in the UK is the Greyhound Derby, first held 1927, now run at Wimbledon, London. There are approximately 87 racetracks in the UK.

Griffith-Joyner, (Delorez) Florence (1959–1998)

US track athlete who won four medals at the 1988 Seoul Olympics, including gold medals in the 100 metres and 200 metres and the sprint relay. Her time in the 200 metres was a world record 21.34

seconds. Two months earlier at the US Trials she had had reduced the 100 metres world record by more than a quarter of a second with a run of 10.49 seconds.

Guscott, Jeremy (1965–)

English rugby union player for **Bath**, England, and the **British Lions**. A fast, elusive centre of prodigious talent, he was a key member of the England side that won three Grand Slams in the Five Nations Championship between 1991 and 1995. He has played on three consecutive British Lions tours since 1989, most memorably in the second Test on the 1997 tour of South Africa when he sealed the series for the Lions with a drop goal.

He won 65 England caps, scoring 30 tries. Only Rory Underwood, with 49 tries from 85 matches, has scored more international tries for England.

gymnastics

Physical exercises, originally for health and training (so called from the way in which men of ancient Greece trained: *gymnos* 'naked'). The *gymnasia* were schools for training competitors for public games. Men's gymnastics includes high bar, parallel bars, horse vault, rings, pommel horse, and floor exercises. Women's gymnastics includes asymmetrical bars, side horse vault, balance beam, and floor exercises. Also popular are sports acrobatics, performed by gymnasts in pairs, trios, or

gymnastics *Gymnast Yuri Chechi of Italy, gold medalist in the 1996 Olympic games, on the rings.*

fours to music, where the emphasis is on dance, balance, and timing, and rhythmic gymnastics, choreographed to music and performed by individuals or six-girl teams, with small hand apparatus such as a ribbon, ball, or hoop. Gymnastics was first revived in 19th-century Germany as an aid to military strength, and was also taken up by educationists including Friedrich Froebel and Johann Pestalozzi, becoming a recognized part of the school curriculum. Today it is a popular spectator sport.

Hagler, Marvin (1954–)
US boxer who was the undisputed world middleweight champion from 1980 to 1987. He won 13 of his 15 World Title fights, losing only to **Sugar Ray Leonard**. Subsequently, he became a movie actor.

hammer
Throwing event in track and field athletics. The hammer is a spherical weight attached to a wire with a handle. The competitors spin the hammer over their heads to gain momentum, within the confines of a circle, and throw it as far as they can, using heel-and-toe turns to build up momentum. The senior men's hammer weighs 7.26 kg/16 lb and may originally have been a blacksmith's hammer. Women and junior men throw lighter implements. The women's hammer event was admitted to the 2000 Olympic Games in Sydney, Australia.

Hampden Park
Scottish football ground, opened in 1903. It is home to the Queen's Park club and the national Scottish team. It plays host to the Scottish FA Cup and League Cup final each year, as well as semi-finals and other matches. It recorded a crowd of 149,547 for the Scotland versus England game in 1937, the largest official attendance for a football match in Britain.

handball
Game resembling **football** but played with the hands instead of the feet. It was popularized in Germany in the late 19th century. The indoor game has seven players in a team; the outdoor version (field handball) has eleven. Indoor handball was introduced as an Olympic event in 1972 for men, and in 1976 for women.

handicapping

Handicapping is the system of adjusting scores that allows people of different abilities or weights to compete on level terms. For example a golfer's handicap is calculated by deducting from the number of strokes taken to play 18 holes from the par for the course. Other sports using handicapping systems include horse racing and polo.

hang-gliding

Technique of unpowered flying using air currents, perfected by US engineer Francis Rogallo in the 1970s. The aeronaut is strapped into a carrier, attached to a sail wing of nylon stretched on an aluminium frame like a paper dart, and jumps into the air from a high place, where updraughts of warm air allow soaring on the thermals.

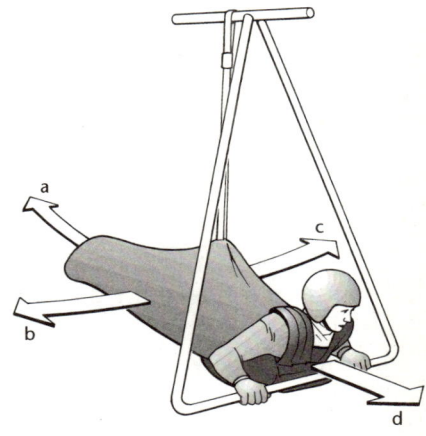

hang-gliding *(a) Pilot moves aft to decrease speed; (b) Pilot's weight right to turn right; (c) Pilot's weight left to turn left; (d) Pilot moves forward to increase speed.*

Hanley, Ellery (1965–)

English **rugby league** player. A strong, highly versatile player equally adept as a forward or a back. He scored 20 tries in 35 internationals for Great Britain, 1984–93. With **Wigan** between 1985 and 1991 he won 16 trophies including the Challenge Cup five times and the Division One Championship three times. In 1994, six years after becoming the first black player to captain Great Britain, he became Great Britain's first black coach.

Harlequins FC

Founded in 1866 as the Hampstead Football Club, the 'Quins' were founder members of the **Rugby Football** Union and play in distinctive quartered shirts. A stylish club with a strong public school, Oxbridge, and 'City' tradition, it developed a hard-nosed professional approach in the 1980s and 1990s that saw it bring the Tetley's Bitter Cup back to the Stoop Memorial Ground twice. Famous Harlequins include Jason Leonard, Brian Moore, and current coach Zinzan Brooke, though the most famous of all is Will **Carling**, one of 21 Harlequins to captain England.

harness racing (trotting or pacing)

Form of **horse racing**, in which the horses are harnessed, pull a light vehicle (sulky) and compete at either a trotting or pacing gait. If a horse breaks the pace and gallops, the driver must start it again.

Hawick FC

A Scottish border **rugby union** club, Hawick has long been a force in Scottish rugby, winning the first Border league in 1901–2, the first Scottish championship 1972–73, and the first Scottish Rugby Union Cup. Famous Hawick players include Colin Deans, Tony Stanger, and Cameron Murray, but the most famous is rugby commentator Bill McLaren.

Headingley

Leeds sports centre, home of the Yorkshire County Cricket Club and Leeds Rugby League Club. The two venues are separated by a large stand. The cricket ground has been a centre for Test matches since 1899. The crowd of 158,000 for the five-day England–Australia Test match at Headingley in 1948 is an English record. Britain's first official Rugby League Test match against New Zealand was at Headingley in 1908. The rugby ground is one of the best in the country and was the first club to install undersoil heating. The main stand is one of the biggest in Rugby League. **See also:** *rugby league.*

Henley Royal Regatta

UK **rowing** festival on the River Thames at Henley, Oxfordshire, inaugurated in 1839. It is as much a social as a sporting occasion. The principal events are the solo Diamond Challenge Sculls and the Grand Challenge Cup, the leading event for eight-oared shells.

The regatta is held in June/July. From 1998 professional rowers were allowed to compete at Henley after the Regatta's stewards had dropped the amateur definition from their rules.

heptathlon
Multi-event athletics discipline for women consisting of seven events over two days: 100-metre hurdles, **high jump**, **shot put**, 200 metres (day one); **long jump**, **javelin**, 800 metres (day two). Points are awarded for performances in each event in the same way as the **decathlon**.

Heysel Stadium disaster
In May 1985, the Champions' Cup Final between **Liverpool** and Juventus was blighted when violent clashes between fans led to a stampede that left 39 Juventus fans crushed to death. Inadequate safety arrangements were blamed, as were English football hooligans. The Heysel stadium in Brussels has now been reopened as the King Baudoin Stadium.

Hickstead
English equestrian centre built in 1960 at the Sussex home of Douglas Bunn (1928–   ), a leading figure and administrator in the horse world. The British Show Jumping Derby has been held there since 1961, as well as many other national and international events.

Higgins, Alex (Gordon) (1949–   )
Northern Irish **snooker** player, born in Belfast, County Antrim. At the age of 23, Higgins became the then youngest player to take the Embassy World Snooker Championship when he defeated John Spencer in 1972. Volatile at times, Higgins was nonetheless a hugely popular figure in the game; his 16–15 victory over Jimmy White in the 1982 World Championship ranks as a classic, and he went on to take the final, beating the Welsh player Ray Reardon. Higgins was also part of the successful Irish team that won three world titles during the 1980s.

high jump

Field event in athletics in which competitors leap over a horizontal crossbar held between rigid uprights at least 3.66 m/12 ft apart. The bar is placed at increasingly higher levels. Elimination occurs after three consecutive failures to clear the bar.

Highland Games

Traditional Scottish outdoor gathering that includes tossing the caber, putting the shot, running, dancing, and bagpipe playing. The most celebrated is the **Braemar** Gathering, held annually in August.

Hill, Damon (1960–)

English **motor-racing** driver. He won the 1996 **Formula 1** World Drivers' Championship. The son of Graham Hill, he began his Formula 1 racing career with Brabham in 1992 before replacing Nigel **Mansell** at Williams, who had used him as a test driver. He won his first Grand Prix in Hungary in 1993. In both 1994 and 1995 he finished as runner-up to Michael Schumacher in the Drivers' Championship. In 1996 he led the championship from start to finish, winning 8 races and finishing 19 points ahead of his nearest rival, though only clinching the championship at the last Grand Prix of the season. He joined the TWR Arrows team for the 1997 season and moved to Jordan in 1998. Also in 1998, he finished in sixth place in the 1998 Formula 1 World Drivers' Championship.

Hill, (Norman) Graham (1929–1975)

English **motor-racing** driver. He won the Dutch Grand Prix in 1962, progressing to the world driver's title in 1962 and 1968. In 1972 he became the first Formula 1 World Champion to win the **Le Mans** Grand Prix d'Endurance (Le Mans 24-Hour Race). He was also the only driver to win the Formula 1 world championship, Le Mans 24-Hour Race, and the Indianapolis 500 Race in his career as a driver. Hill started his Formula 1 career with Lotus in 1958, went to BRM 1960–66, returned to Lotus 1967–69, moved to Brabham 1970–72, and formed his own team, Embassy Shadow, 1973–75. He was killed in an air crash. His son Damon **Hill** won his first Grand Prix in 1993, making them the first father and son to both win a Grand Prix.

Hillsborough disaster
Disaster on 15 April 1989 at the Hillsborough **football** ground in Sheffield in which 96 Liverpool fans were killed during an FA Cup match between **Liverpool** and Nottingham Forest. The deaths occurred when Liverpool fans were crushed on the overcrowded Leppings Lane stand.

Hinault, Bernard (1954–   )
French cyclist. One of four men to have won the **Tour de France** five times (1978, 1979, 1981, 1982, and 1985).

hockey
Game played with hooked sticks and a small, solid ball, the object being to hit the ball into the goal. It is played between two teams, each of not more than 11 players. Hockey has been an Olympic sport since 1908 for men and since 1980 for women. In North America it is known as 'field hockey', to distinguish it from ice hockey. The game is divided into two 35-minute periods; it is controlled by two umpires, one for each half of the field.

hockey, street
Form of **hockey** played on roller skates. At one time played mostly on streets in the USA, it is now played in indoor arenas. It rapidly increased in popularity in the UK in the late 1980s.

Honourable Company of Edinburgh Golfers
Oldest **golf** club in the world. It was formed in 1744 as the Gentleman Golfers of Edinburgh and played over the Leith links. The current club name was adopted in 1759. It drew up the first set of golf rules, which were later accepted by the ruling body of the Royal and Ancient Club of St Andrews. The club moved to Musselburgh in 1836 and, in 1891, to its present home in Muirfield. It has staged the British **Open** 14 times between 1892 and 1992.

Hoogenband, Pieter van den (1978–   )
Dutch swimmer. At the 1999 European Championships in Istanbul,

Turkey, Hoogenband joined the world's elite swimmers by winning gold medals in six events: the 50-metre, 100-metre, and 200-metre freestyle events, the 4 x 100-metre freestyle relay, the 4 x 100-metre medley relay, and the non-Olympic 50-metre butterfly event. He was denied an unprecedented seventh European crown when his 4 x 200-metre freestyle relay team was disqualified after a false start. At the Sydney Olympic Games 2000 he won bronze in the 2 x 400-metre freestyle relay, the gold medal in the 100-metre and 200-metre freestyle events, and a bronze in the 50-metre freestyle.

horse racing

Sport of racing mounted or driven (hitched) horses. Three popular forms exist:

- *flat racing*, in which thoroughbred horses are guided over a flat course by a rider called a jockey;

- *harness racing*, in which a driver in a two-wheeled cart called a sulky drives a horse in one of two gaits: pacing (both legs on the same side are off the ground at the same time); trotting (diagonal legs are off the ground at the same time);

- and the *steeplechase*, in which horses race around a course that has numerous obstacles over which the horse must jump. These may include fences, barred jumps, hedges, stone walls, and water.

❛ Some people work to earn enough money to have fun. I enjoy the work best of all. ❜

Lester Piggott, British jockey, 1970.

---

hurdling

The hurdles are sprint events where competitors must also clear 10 barriers (the hurdles). Most athletic competitions have two hurdles events: the 110-metre hurdles (100 metres for women) and the 400-metre hurdles. The men's high hurdles are run over barriers 107 cm/42.13 in high, while the 400-metre barriers measure 91 cm/ 35.83 in; the sprint hurdles for women are 84 cm/33.07 in high and the 400-metre

barriers measure 76 cm/
29.92 in. Great sprint
hurdlers include Greg
Foster and Renaldo
Nehemiah, while the
400-metre hurdles'
dominant force was
Edwin Moses.

hurling

Irish national game and
the fastest field sport in
the world, played by

hurdling   *Colin Jackson of Great Britain in the 110 m
hurdles at the 1996 Olympic Games.*

teams of 15 men a side with a ball and sticks. Hurling can be dated
back over 2,000 years in the annals of the Celts. Since the founding of
Cumann Lúthchleas Gael (the **Gaelic Athletic Association**) in 1884 the
sport has continued to gain in popularity, both nationally and internationally. Hurling is played on a pitch usually 137 m/150 yd long and
82 m/90 yd wide. The object is to drive the 'sliotar' (ball), 25 cm/10 in
in circumference, through erect posts at opposite ends of the pitch.
Each player uses a wooden hurley or 'caman', usually 1.07 m/3.5 ft
long, to propel the sliotar around the playing area. The erect goalposts
stand 6.4 m/21 ft apart and are usually about 6.4 m/21 ft high. There
is a crossbar 2.4 m/8 ft from the ground. Hitting the ball over the crossbar scores a point and a shot under scores a goal.

Hurst, Geoff(rey Charles) (1941–   )

English football player who scored three goals in England's 4–2 victory in the 1966 World Cup final at Wembley, the only time a
hat-trick has been scored in a World Cup final. A virtual unknown
internationally before the tournament began, having only made his
full England debut two months earlier, he was surprisingly preferred
to the prolific scoring Jimmy Greaves in the competition's final
stages. He went on to make a total of 49 appearances for England,
scoring 24 goals. He was knighted in 1998.

IAAF (International Amateur Athletic Federation)
Seventeen national athletics federations founded the IAAF in 1912 to provide a governing body that would standardize rules, technical equipment, world records etc. The **International Olympic Committee** ran the **Olympic Games**, but with the growth of televised sport, the role of the IAAF increased and it has responsibility for the World Championships, **World Cup**, World Youth Championships, World Indoor Championships, race walking, cross country, Grand Prix, and other competitions. Over 200 federations are now members of the IAAF, whose headquarters are in Monaco.

Ibrox disaster

There have been two Ibrox disasters. The first, in 1902 at a Scotland– England international, saw 25 fans left dead after a new stand collapsed. In 1971, the second tragedy saw 66 fans trampled to death and another 100 badly injured at the end of a Rangers–Celtic 'Old Firm' derby. It is believed the incident occurred when two boys bent over to pick something up in a stairwell, tripping up fans coming behind. As more fans tried to get off the terraces, panic and a deadly crush ensued.

> The worst soccer tragedy was in 1982 where at least 320 spectators at the Spartak Moscow-Haarlem UEFA Cup tie died as fans leaving the Lenin stadium in Moscow poured back in after a late goal, causing a stampede.

ice hockey

A game played on ice between two teams of six. It was developed in Canada from field hockey or bandy. Players, who wear skates and protective clothing, use a curved stick to advance the puck (a rubber disk) and shoot it at the opponents' goal, a netted cage, guarded by the goalie. The other positions are the left and right defencemen and the left wing, centre, and right wing. The latter three are offensive players. The team with

ice hockey *Russia's ice hockey team compete against Finland in the 1998 Winter Olympics. Russia's Zelepukin (number 25) causes problems for Finland.*

the most goals scored at the end of the three 20-minute periods wins; an overtime period may be played if a game ends in a tie. The standard hockey rink is 200 ft/61 m long and 85 ft/26 m wide, with rounded corners and enclosed by a board wall 4 ft/1.3 m high. The goals are centred on a red line that crosses the rink 10 ft/ 3 m from each end of the rink. In front of each goal is a rectangular area called the crease, in which the goalie can operate freely, since other players cannot score from that area.

ice hockey, history of

Ice hockey is believed to have been first introduced in Canada in the 1850s, with the first game being played in Kingston, Ontario. The first rules were drawn up at McGill University, Montreal. The governing body is the International Ice Hockey Federation (IIHF), founded in 1908. Canada's first hockey league, the Amateur Hockey Association, was formed in 1885. In 1893, Lord Stanley, Canada's governor general gave a cup to be awarded to Canada's champion amateur team. By 1912, there were various professional leagues, and a playoff for the championship was inaugurated. The winner was awarded the **Stanley Cup**, which has since become the symbol of professional hockey's championship. The National Hockey League (NHL), founded in 1917, became the dominant professional league and now consists of two conferences, each with two divisions. Ice hockey has been included in the **Olympic Games** since 1920 when it was part of the Summer Games programme. Since 1924 it has been part of the **Winter Olympics**.

Iditarod
A deserted mining town in western Alaska, USA, that gives its name to the annual 1,868-km/1,160-mi-long Iditarod dogsled race from Anchorage to Nome, inaugurated in 1973.

Following an old mail route, the race commemorates a 1925 medical mission to Nome during a diphtheria epidemic. Traversing the Alaska Range and running along the Yukon River and Bering Sea coast, it begins in March and attracts some 50 drivers and teams. The winner usually takes 10–11 days to complete the course. **See also:** *dogsled racing.*

Indianapolis Raceway
US motor-sport circuit, built in 1910 following the success of **Brooklands** in the UK. The Indianapolis 500 is staged here at the end of May each year as part of the Memorial Day weekend. It will stage a **Formula 1** Grand Prix for the first time in the year 2000.

The circuit is 2.5 miles/4 km long and is rectangular with the four corners joined at slightly banked corners. The original circuit was made out of bricks, hence its nickname the 'Brickyard'.

Indurain, Miguel Larraya (1964–)
Spanish cyclist. The first rider to win the **Tour de France** in five consecutive years (1991–95), Indurain's dominance of the Tour was founded on his mastery of the time-trial stages and his endurance in the mountains.

Inter Milan FC
Formed in 1908, Inter Milan is one of Italy's top teams and has notched up an impressive 13 league titles, two European Cups, three Coppa Italia titles, three UEFA Cups, one Super cup, and one World Club Cup. The stadium is named after Guiseppe Meazza, the club's

all-time top goal scorer with 248 shots on target. Other famous Inter stars include Guiseppe Bergomi, Christian Vieri, and Dennis Bergkamp.

International Olympic Committee (IOC)

The IOC was founded in 1894 by Pierre de Coubertin, and acts as the umbrella for the Olympic movement worldwide. It owns the legal rights to the Olympic symbols, flag, motto, anthem, and **Olympic Games**, and its primary role is the organization of the summer and winter games. The president of the IOC is Juan Antonio **Samaranch** of Spain.

Isle of Man TT (Tourist Trophy) Races

The TT races first took place in 1907 when the laws of England and Wales at that time did not allow roads to be closed to hold races, and speed limits were strictly enforced. However an Act of Parliament allowed Manx roads to be closed for racing trials: when this was extended to cover bikes, the TT races were born. They are held in May/June each year. The TT mountain course measures 37.73 mi/60.72 km and was first used in 1911, with major races then involving six laps of the course. Bikes are categorized according to engine capacity, with races for Formula 1, Senior, and Junior machines as well as sidecar combinations.

javelin

Spear used in athletics events. The men's javelin is about 260 cm/8.5 ft long, weighing 800 g/28 oz; the women's is 230 cm/7.5 ft long, and weighs 600 g/21 oz. It is thrown from a scratch line at the end of a run-up. The centre of gravity on the men's javelin was altered in 1986 to reduce the vast distances (90 m/100 yd) that were being thrown.

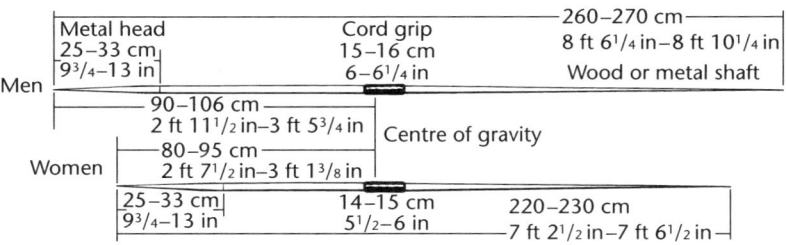

javelin *The javelin must be without mobile parts. The cord grip is around the centre of gravity. The minimum weight for men is 800 g/1.8 lb and for women 600 g/1.3 lb.*

Jenkins, Neil Roger (1971–)

Welsh **rugby union** player. A brilliant goal kicker, he made his international debut in 1991 against England. One of the stars of the triumphant **British Lions** tour of South Africa in 1997, he scored 41 of the Lions' 59 points in the three-test series. By the end of the 1998 Five Nations championship he had scored 594 points in 57 games, 290 more than any other Welshman has achieved. At the end of the 1999 Five Nations he had scored 764 points in 66 internationals (63 for Wales; 3 for the British Lions). In the same competition he set new Welsh records for the most points in a championship season (64) and the most points in a single Five Nations match (22). In Wales's **Rugby World Cup** match against Samoa at Cardiff in October 1999, he overtook Michael Lynagh's record career total of 911 points to become the highest international points scorer of all time. He became the record all-time points scorer in the **Six Nations Championship** (formerly the Five Nations), finishing the 2000 tournament with a career total of 332 points. The previous record holder was Gavin Hastings with 288 points.

CAREER HIGHLIGHTS

international appearances
80 (including 3 for the British Lions)

tries
9

penalties
231 (including 13 for the British Lions)

conversions
116 (including 1 for the British Lions)

drop goals
5

total points
985 (including 41 for the British Lions)

club honours (Pontypridd)
Welsh League 1997

SWALEC Cup
1997

Jockey Club

Governing body of English **horseracing** until 1993, when the British Horseracing Board was formed. The Jockey Club still oversees licensing and regulation. It was founded in about 1750 at the Star and Garter, Pall Mall, London.

Johnson, Ben (1961–   )

Canadian athlete. Born in Jamaica, he moved to Canada in 1976 to train for the 100-metre sprint. Having won numerous awards and been inducted into the Canadian Amateur Sports hall of fame in 1988, at the Seoul Olympic Games in that same year, he tested positive for stanozolol, a banned performance enhancing drug, after winning the 100-metre sprint in a world record time of 9.97 sec. He was the first ever athlete to break the 10 sec barrier. He was stripped of his gold medal, which was then awarded to the second-placed Carl Lewis. Johnson's ban was lifted in September 1990 but when he failed a second dope test in 1993 he was banned for life.

Johnson, Michael (1967–)

US track and field athlete. At Atlanta in 1996 Johnson became the first man in Olympic history to win gold medals in both 200 metres and 400 metres. In the 200-metre final he set a new world record of 19.32 seconds and finished .36 seconds ahead of the second placed athlete, a margin of victory only bettered by Jesse **Owens** at the 1936 Olympics. In 1995 Johnson completed an unprecedented 200 metre–400 metre double at the World Championships, and in 1997 won his third 400-metre World Championship title in a row. In the course of winning his fourth consecutive 400-metre title at the World Championships in Seville, Spain, in August 1999, he broke the world record with a run of 43.18 seconds. Johnson also won another gold medal as a member of the victorious US 4 x 400-metre relay team. In the 2000 Olympic Games in Sydney he became the only man to succesfully defend the 400-metre Olympic title.

CAREER HIGHLIGHTS

Olympic Games
gold 200 metres, 400 metres, 1996; gold 4 x 100-metre relay 1992

World Championships
gold 200 metres 1991, 1995; gold 400 metres 1993, 1995, 1997, 1999; gold 4 x 400-metre relay 1993, 1995, 1999

Jordan, Michael Jeffrey (1963–   )

US **basketball** player. Named by the US magazine *Sports Illustrated* as the 'Best Basketball Player of the 20th Century' (1999), he played for the **Chicago Bulls** from 1984, and led them to National Basketball Association (NBA) championship wins in 1991, 1992, 1993, 1996,

1997, and 1998. During the 1986–87 season he scored 3,000 points; he was only the second player in NBA history to do so. Jordan led the league in scoring for a record ten times. Only Kareem Abdul-Jabbar and Wilt Chamberlain to date scored more than Jordan's 29,277 career points in the NBA. No other player with over 10,000 points could match Jordan's career average of 31.5 points per game. In a total of 179 play-off games he scored a record 5,987 points at an average of 33.4. No other player in the history of the NBA play-offs has achieved a points-per-game average over 30.

Jordan *Basketball star Michael Jordan dunks the ball unchallenged in a game against the Atlanta Hawks.*

Joyner-Kersee, Jackie (1962–)

US track and field athlete. One of the greatest female athletes in history. At the **Olympic Games** in the **heptathlon** she won a silver medal in 1984 and gold medals in 1988 and 1992; in the **long jump** she won a gold medal in 1988 and a bronze in 1992.

judo

From the Japanese *ju do*, 'gentle way', a form of wrestling of Japanese origin. The two combatants wear loose-fitting, belted jackets and trousers to facilitate holds, and falls are broken by a square mat; when one has established a painful hold that the other cannot break, the latter signifies surrender by slapping the ground with a free hand. Degrees of proficiency are indicated by the colour of the belt: for novices, white, then yellow, orange (2 degrees), green (2 degrees), blue (2 degrees), brown (2 degrees), then black (Dan grades; 10 degrees, of which 1st to 5th Dan wear black belts, 6th to 9th wear red and white, and 10th wears solid red). Judo became an Olympic sport in 1964. The world championship was first held in 1956 for men, in 1980 for women; it is now contested biennially.

jujitsu (or jujutsu)
Traditional Japanese form of self-defence; the modern form is **judo**.

karate

From the Japanese 'empty hand', one of the martial arts. Karate is a type of unarmed combat derived from *kempo*, a form of the Chinese Shaolin boxing. It became popular in the West in the 1930s.

Karpov, Anatoly Yevgenyevich (1951–)

Russian **chess** player. He succeeded **Bobby Fischer** of the USA as world champion in 1975, and held the title until losing to **Gary Kasparov** in 1985. He lost to Kasparov again in 1990. In January 1998 Karpov won the FIDE World Chess Championship defeating Viswanathan Anand of India in the final. He lost the FIDE World Chess title in 1999 to Russian Alexander Khalifman.

karting or go-karting

Miniature motor racing with low-framed, light-chassis cars; it originated in the USA about 1955. In competitive racing, different formulas exist. Standard production two-stroke engines are capable of providing speeds of approximately 240 kph/150 mph.

Kasparov, Gary Kimovich (1963–)

Born Garri Weinstein, Soviet **chess** player. When he beat his compatriot Anatoly **Karpov** to win the world title in 1985, he was the youngest-ever champion at 22 years 210 days. In October 1995, he beat Viswanathan Anand in the Professional Chess Association championship.

Keegan, (Joseph) Kevin (1951–)

English **football** player and football manager. He was Footballer of the Year and PFA Player of the Year in 1976, European Footballer of the Year in 1978 and 1979, and PFA Player of the Year in 1982. He became manager of Newcastle United in 1992. In February 1999 he was appointed coach of the England team on a part-time basis, whilst continuing at Fulham, the team he led to the 1998–99 Second Division Championship. In May 1999 he parted company with Fulham after deciding to accept the England manager's job on a full-time basis, and signed a contract to coach England until the end of the 2002 **World Cup** finals. He steered England through to the 2000 European Championships but the team only achieved qualification after narrowly defeating Scotland and performed poorly in the competition itself. Keegan resigned as manager in October 2000 following England's defeat by Germany in a World Cup qualifier.

> ❝ I enjoyed myself playing for Scunthorpe. What more can you ask for? ❞
>
> **Kevin Keegan**, 1973.

kendo
Japanese armed martial art in which combatants fence with bamboo replicas of samurai swords. Masks and padding are worn for protection. The earliest recorded reference to kendo is from AD 789.

Kentucky Derby
Established as a race to rival the Epson Derby, the Kentucky Derby was first run in May 1875 at the Churchill Downs track, Louisville, Kentucky, but it was not until 1902 that it achieved a greater prominence than a regional race, when the track's new owner, Colonel Matt J Winn, encouraged the great owners of the day to enter their horses in the Kentucky Derby. The Derby, run over one-and-a-quarter miles, is part of a week-long festival, attracting crowds of over 100,000 spectators.

Khan, Jahangir (1963–) and Khan, Jansher (1969–)
Pakistani **squash** players. Jahangir won the World Open championship six times 1981–85 and 1988, and was World **Amateur**

champion in 1979, 1983, and 1985. His nephew, Jansher, has won the World Open squash championship a record eight times since 1987. Jansher became Asian Junior Champion in 1985. Two years later, aged only 18, he defeated his uncle, the world number one Jahangir Khan, in the final of the World Open championships. Since 1989, a year after Jahangir regained the title, he has lost the tournament only once. He has won the British Open five times in succession since ending Jahangir's record ten year unbeaten run in 1992.

King, Billie Jean (1943–   )

US **tennis** player. She won a record 20 **Wimbledon** titles 1961–79 and 39 **Grand Slam** titles, and fought for equal treatment and equal pay for women tennis players. In 1973 she formed the Women's Tennis Association and the Players' Union. In 1974, with Olympic swimmer Donna de Varona and others, she created the Women's Sports Foundation to support and promote women in sport. When she arrived on the professional circuit, King brought with her a desire to pursue equality for women players, a desire that would dominate her career. Her first Wimbledon title was the doubles with Karen Hantze in 1961, and her last, also doubles, with Martina **Navratilova** in 1979. She won the Wimbledon singles title six times,

---

CAREER HIGHLIGHTS

Winbledon
singles: 1966–68, 1972–73, 1975; doubles: 1961–62, 1965, 1967–68, 1970–73, 1979; mixed: 1967, 1871, 1973–1974

US Open
singles: 1967, 1971–72, 1974; doubles: 1964, 1967, 1974, 1978, 1980; mixed: 1967, 1971, 1973, 1976

French Open
singles: 1972; doubles: 1972; mixed: 1967, 1970

Australian Open
singles: 1968; mixed: 1968

the US Open singles title four times, the French Open once, and the Australian Open once. Her 39 Grand Slam wins at singles and doubles are third only to Navratilova and Margaret Court.

Klammer, Franz (1953–)

Austrian skier. He won a record 25 World Cup downhill races 1974–85, plus one win in the combined event. He was an Olympic gold medallist in 1976. He was the combined world champion in 1974, and the World Cup downhill champion 1975–78 and 1983. He was the most successful Austrian skier in World Cup competition until February 2000 when **Hermann Maier** achieved his 27th victory.

Knox-Johnston, Robin (1939–)

English yachtsman. In 1969, in the *Suhaili*, he became the first person to sail non-stop, single-handed around the world. The holder of the 1986 British Sailing Trans Atlantic Record, he has also won the Round Britain Race in both the two-man and crewed sections. Co-skipper with Peter Blake on the *Enza NZ*, he achieved the world's fastest circumnavigation under sail in 1994. He was knighted in 1995.

Korbut, Olga Valentinovna (1955–)

Soviet **gymnast**. She attracted world attention at the 1972 **Olympic Games** with her lively floor routine, winning three gold medals for the team, beam, and floor exercises.

korfball

Korfball is a mixed team sport, with teams of eight (equal numbers of males and females) that play both in attack and defence: the squads swap over after two goals. A form of handball, it is played on a pitch measuring 90 m x 40 m/296 ft x 1311 ft and divided into three zones across the width. The object is to score by playing the ball into a basket on a pole. One is mounted one at either end of the field.

Kristiansen, Ingrid (1956–   )
Norwegian athlete, an outstanding long-distance runner of the 5,000 metres, the 10,000 metres, the marathon, and cross-country races. She has won all the world's leading marathons. In 1986 she knocked 45.68 seconds off the world 10,000 metres record. She was the world cross-country champion in 1988 and won the London marathon 1984–85 and 1987–88.

kung fu
Chinese art of unarmed combat, one of the martial arts. It is practised in many forms, the most popular being *wing chun*, 'beautiful springtime'. The basic principle is to use attack as a form of defence. Kung fu dates from the 6th century, and was popularized in the West by the film actor Bruce Lee in the 1970s.

Kwik Cricket
Trade name for a form of cricket devised for children, popularized in the 1980s. It is played with a soft ball and all players get a chance to bat and bowl.

lacrosse

Canadian ball game, adopted from the Native American, and named after a fancied resemblance of the lacrosse stick (crosse) to a bishop's crosier. Thongs across the curved end of the crosse form a pocket to carry the small rubber ball. The field is approximately 100 m/ 110 yd long and a minimum of 55 m/60 yd wide in the men's game, which is played with 10 players per side; the women's field is larger, and there are 12 players per side. The goals are just less than 2 m/6 ft square, with loose nets. The world championship was first held in 1967 for men, and in 1969 for women.

lacrosse *Players jump for the ball at the start of a game of lacrosse in 1925.*

Laker, Jim (James Charles) (1922–1986)

English cricketer who, in the 4th Test against Australia at Manchester in 1956, returned figures of 9–37 and 10–53 to become the first bowler to take 19 wickets in a Test or first-class match, and to take 10 wickets in a Test match innings. A tall, right-arm off-spinner with a classical action, he took 193 wickets in 46 Tests, 1948–59, at an average of 21.24.

Lara, Brian (1969–   )

Trinidadian cricketer. A left-handed batsman, he plays first-class **cricket** for Trinidad and Tobago and for Warwickshire. In April 1994 he broke the world individual Test batting record with an innings of 375 against England, and 50 days later he broke the world record for an individual innings in first-class cricket with an unbeaten 501 for Warwickshire against Durham. In February 2000, after two years in the position, Lara stepped down as West Indies captain. Under his captaincy the West Indies had a record of five wins, one draw, and nine defeats.

Lauda, Niki (Nikolas Andreas) (1949–   )

Austrian motor-racing driver who won the **Formula 1** World Championship in 1975, 1977, and 1984. He was also runner-up in 1976, just six weeks after having a serious accident at Nurburgring, Germany.

Lawn Tennis Association (LTA)

The governing body of **tennis** in the UK, the LTA was formed in 1888 and was responsible for drawing up the laws of lawn tennis, which have changed little over the years. Despite its name, the LTA is responsible for organizing hard-court competitions, and owns Queen's Club, London (where its heaadquarters are located); however, the LTA has no influence in the organization of **Wimbledon**, the game's main grass-court tournament. It also has responsibility for selecting and managing teams for major tournaments such as the **Davis Cup**, running rating tournaments at senior and junior levels, and the national tennis centre at Bisham Abbey.

Leeds United FC

Formed in 1908 when Leeds City was kicked out of the Football League for making illegal payments, United's glory days were the 1960s under the generalship of manager Don Revie, though its finest players were the Milburn brothers and the giant John Charles. After Revie became England manager, Leeds' fortunes declined though the appointment of Howard Wilkinson, then George Graham, and David O'Leary brought silverware back to Elland Road.

Leicester RFC
The Tigers were one of England's dominant teams of the late 20th century, along with **Bath**, and have recently won the 1998–99 and 1999–2000 Allied-Dunbar League titles. The Welford Road club was formed in 1880 and has won a host of titles. Wearers of the Tigers' red, green, and white-hooped shirts have included Peter Wheeler, Paul Dodge, Dean Richards, and Rory Underwood.

Le Mans
Motor racing circuit where the annual endurance 24-hour race (established in 1923) for sports cars and their prototypes is held at the Sarthe circuit. It is linked to Paris by a high-speed rail system.

Leonard, Sugar Ray (Ray Charles) (1956–   )
US boxer. In 1988 he became the first man to have won world titles at five officially recognized weights. In 1976 he was Olympic light-welterweight champion; he won his first professional title in 1979 when he beat Wilfred Benitez for the World Boxing Council (WBC) welterweight title. He later won titles at junior middleweight (World Boxing Association; WBA version) 1981, middleweight (WBC) 1987, light-heavyweight (WBC) 1988, and super-middleweight (WBC) 1988. In 1989 he drew with Thomas Hearns. He retired in 1992, but made a defeated comeback in 1997.

Lewis, Carl (Frederick Carlton) (1961–   )
US track and field athlete. He won nine gold medals and one silver in four successive **Olympic Games**. At the 1984 Olympic Games he equalled the performance of Jesse Owens, winning gold medals in the 100 metres and 200 metres, 400-metre relay, and long jump. He officially ended his career in 1997 at the age of 36. In November 1999 he was voted 'Sportsman of the Century' by the **International Olympic Committee** (IOC), and in December 1999 the US magazine *Sports Illustrated* named him the 'Best Olympian of the 20th

Century'.

At the 1988 Olympics, Lewis repeated his golds in the 100 metres and long jump, winning a silver in the 200 metres. At the 1992 Olympics he again won gold in the long jump. He also anchored the USA's records-breaking 4 x 400 metre relay team. His long jump gold at the Atlanta Olympics was his fourth consecutive long jump title and his ninth gold medal in all, equaling the achievement of the great Finnish athlete Paavo Nurmi.

CAREER HIGHLIGHTS

Olympic Games
gold 100 metres 1984, 1988; gold 200 metres 1984; gold 4 x 100-metre relay 1984, 1992; gold long jump 1984, 1988, 1992, 1996; silver 200 metres 1988

World Championships
gold 100 metres 1983, 1991; gold 4 x 100-metre relay 1983, 1987, 1991; gold long jump 1983, 1987; silver 100 metres 1987; silver long jump 1991

Lewis, Lennox Claudius (1966–   )

English boxer who won the WBC world heavyweight title in 1992, becoming the first British boxer to do so this century. He was awarded the title when the reigning champion, Riddick Bowe, refused to fight him. After defending the title successfully for nearly two years, he lost to Oliver McCall in September 1994. However, he regained the title in February 1997. On 13 March 1999 at Madison Square Garden, New York City, in what was undoubtedly the biggest fight of his professional career, he fought a controversial 12 round draw with the WBA and IBF world champion Evander Holyfield of the USA. Lewis landed considerably more punches, and most observers, fans, and experts alike, felt that he had done more than enough to win; however, one of the three judges gave the verdict to Holyfield, another scored it a draw. In the November 1999 rematch, Lewis won the bout, held at Las Vegas, on a unanimous points decision.

Lewis is the first British-born undisputed world heavyweight champion since Bob Fitzimmons, who held the title from 1879 to 1899. However he subsequently lost his WBA title in court over a breach of contract. He successfully defended his WBC and IBF world titles against South African born US boxer Francois Bota in London, England, on 15 July 2000. In 1999 he was voted 'Sports Personality of the Year' by the British Broadcasting Corporation (BBC).

CAREER HIGHLIGHTS

professional record (1989–)
fights 39; wins 37(29 within the distance),draws 1, defeats 1

Olympic super-heavyweight champion
1988

WBC heavyweight champion
1992–94, 1997–

WBA world heavyweight champion
1999–2000

IBF world heavyweight champion
1999–

Liddell, Eric Henry (1902–1945)

Known as 'the Flying Scotsman'. Scottish athlete and missionary. At the 1924 Olympics in Paris he won the gold medal in the 400 metres in a world record time of 47.6 seconds. In 1925 he went to China to work as a Scottish Congregational Church missionary. During World War II he was interned by the Japanese at Weihsien camp in China, where he died. He would have been the favourite to win the 100 metres at the Paris Olympics had he not refused to take part on religious grounds because the heats were to be run on a Sunday. Instead, he won the bronze medal in the 200 metres. The story of his athletic triumphs was told in the film *Chariots of Fire* (1981).

Lillee, Dennis Keith (1949–)

Australian cricketer. He is regarded as the best fast bowler of his generation. He made his Test debut in the 1970–71 season and subsequently played for his country 70 times. Lillee took 355 wickets in Test cricket. He played Sheffield Shield cricket for Western

Australia and at the end of his career made a comeback with Tasmania.

Lineker, Gary (1960–   )

English footballer. He scored over 250 goals in 550 games for Leicester, **Everton**, **Barcelona**, and **Tottenham**. With 48 goals in 80 internationals he failed by one goal to equal Bobby **Charlton's** record of 49 goals for England. Lineker was elected Footballer of the Year in 1986 and 1992, and was leading scorer at the 1986 **World Cup** finals. In 1993 he moved to Japan to play for Nagoya Grampus Eight but retired a year later.

Liverpool FC

Liverpool FC was formed in 1878 when **Everton** moved from Anfield to a new ground and it was suggested to Anfield's owner that a new team be set up. Its subsequent record – 18 league titles, five **FA Cups**, five League Cups, 13 Charity Shields, two UEFA Cups, and a European Super Cup – makes Liverpool a giant of the English football game. Favourites at the Kop (one of the enclosures) include **Kenny Dalglish**, Ian Rush, Michael Owen, Graeme Souness, Tommy Smith, and legendary manager Bill Shankly, a product of the 'boot room' (the club's backroom staff).

Llanelli RFC

Llanelli RFC celebrated its centenary in 1972, only for research to suggest the club was actually formed in 1875; the first recorded game was in 1876 and the ground at Stradey Park was acquired in 1879. The club has produced some great players – Phil Bennett, father and son Derek and Scott Quinnell, J J Williams, Delme Thomas, and Ieuan Evans – and has achieved some notable triumphs. It has won the Welsh Challenge Cup 11 times and was the only side – club or international – to beat the **All Blacks** during their 1972–73 tour.

Lomu, Jonah (1975–   )

New Zealand **rugby union** wing three-quarter of Tongan descent who made a phenomenal impact in the 1995 Rugby World Cup in

South Africa when he scored seven tries including four in the semi-final against England. At 1.96 m/6ft 5 in tall and weighing 118 kg/18.5 stone, but with great acceleration, he was stopped only by South African players in the final. In January 1997 he was diagnosed as suffering from a career-threatening kidney condition, but later in the year he made a successful comeback and in 1998 helped New Zealand to the win in the inaugural Commonwealth Games Rugby Sevens in Kuala Lumpur, Malaysia. He was the leading try scorer at the 1999 **Rugby World Cup** tournament with eight tries, bringing his total to an unprecedented fifteen World Cup tries. **See also** *All Blacks, the.*

London Wasps RFC
Named because of the vogue at that time for giving sports clubs animal names (there is also a Preston Grasshoppers RFC and a Centaurs FC!) Wasps was founded in 1867, though its profile was not particularly high – the first England cap for a Wasps player was not won until 1948. Wasps' revival in the later years of the 20th century coincided with the arrival of talented players like Maurice Colcough, props Paul Rendall and Jeff Probyn and half backs Rob Andrew (England's highest points scorer) and Steve Bates. The clubs thrived after rugby went open, winning the first League title 1996–97, and the Tetley's Bitter Cup in 1999 and 2000 under the leadership of **Lawrence Dallaglio**.

long jump
Field event in athletics in which competitors sprint up to and leap from a takeoff board into a sandpit measuring 9 m/29.53 ft in length. The takeoff board is 1 m/3.28 ft from the landing area. Each competitor usually has six attempts, and the winner is the one with the longest jump.

Lord's
Cricket ground in St John's Wood, London. One of England's test-match grounds and the headquarters of one of cricket's governing bodies, the **Marylebone Cricket Club** (**MCC**), since 1788 when the

MCC was formed following the folding of the White Conduit Club. The ground is named after Yorkshireman Thomas Lord (1757–1832) who developed the first site at Dorset Square in 1787. He moved the ground to a field at North Bank, Regent's Park, in 1811, and in 1814 developed the ground at its present site at St John's Wood. Lord's is also the home of Middlesex County Cricket Club. The MCC on 28 September 1998 voted in favour of admitting women for the first time in its 211-year history.

Los Angeles Lakers
Formed in 1948 as the Minneapolis Lakers, the franchise moved to California in 1960 and now plays from the Staples centre, with 12 NBA titles to their credit. The Lakers' top players include Kareem Abdul-Jabaar, Elgin Baylor, and Earvin 'Magic' Johnson.

Louis, Joe (1914–1981)
Assumed name of Joseph Louis Barrow, US boxer, nicknamed 'the Brown Bomber'. He was world heavyweight champion 1937–49 and made a record 25 successful defences (a record for any weight).

luge
A one- or two-person racing sled, on which riders lie face up. Luges are raced by both men and women in the Winter Olympics.

McEnroe, John Patrick
(1959–)

US **tennis** player whose brash behaviour and fiery temper on court dominated the men's game in the early 1980s. He was three times winner of **Wimbledon**, in 1981, and 1983–1984. He also won three successive **US Open** titles 1979–81 and again in 1984. A fine doubles player, McEnroe also won ten **Grand Slam** titles, seven in partnership with Peter Fleming.

After his retirement, he became a tennis commentator for television, with his

McEnroe *John McEnroe at Wimbledon. He is as much renowned for his fiery temper as for his brilliant tennis.*

CAREER HIGHLIGHTS

Wimbledon
singles: 1981, 1983–84; doubles: 1979, 1981, 1983–84, 1992

US Open
singles: 1979–81, 1984; doubles: 1979, 1981, 1983, 1989

French Open
mixed doubles: 1977

Grand Prix Masters
singles: 1979, 1984, 1985; doubles: 1979–85

notoriously outspoken remarks proving very popular with viewers in both the USA and the UK.

McRae, Colin (1968–   )

Scottish rally driver who in 1995, driving a Subaru Impreza, became the first ever British driver to win the world rally championship. At 27 years old he was also the youngest ever champion. In 1994 he had become the first British driver since Roger Clark (1939–1998) in 1976 to win the **RAC Rally**, a race he won again in 1995 and 1997. In 1998 he announced that he would drive for Ford from the following year. McRae first came to the fore in 1991, when he gained the first of two consecutive British Rally Championship titles. He won his first world championship race in 1993 and by the start of the 2000 championship had achieved a career total of 26 victories.

Madison Square Garden

Venue in New York, built as a boxing arena and also used for concerts. The current 'Garden' is the fourth to bear the name and staged its first boxing match in 1968. It is situated over Pennsylvania Station on 7th Avenue, New York City, and has a capacity of 20,000. The first 'Garden' had its roots in the 1870s when an Irishman called Gilmore gave concerts from a disused railway depot in Madison Square Park. It became known as Gilmore's Garden but when the former owner, circus proprietor Barnum, took it over again in 1880 he renamed it Madison Square Garden.

Maier, Hermann (1972–   )

Austrian skier who in 2000 became the first person to win the men's World Cup downhill, Giant Slalom, Super G, and overall titles, in the same season. He came to international prominence in 1998, winning the Giant Slalom and Super G, gold medals at the Winter Olympic Games, and winning the Giant Slalom, Super G and overall World Cup titles. In 1999 he won the Giant Slalom and Super G gold medals at the Alpine World Championships, and gained the Super G World Cup title. During the 1999–2000 season he broke the Austrian record of 26 World Cup victories set by Franz **Klammer**.

Manchester United FC

Football team in England. Old Trafford is a shrine to United fans the world over, with Alex **Ferguson** and Matt **Busby** as its high priests. Formed in 1878 as Newton Heath LYR, it changed its name to Manchester United in 1902. The club has amassed countless honours including 10 FA Cup wins, 10 Charity Shields, the League Cup, two European Champions Cups, and the Cup Winners Cup. The club has known tragedy with the **Munich air disaster**, and great players in the form of David Beckham, Bobby **Charlton**, Mark Hughes, and George **Best**.

Manchester United FC *Ryan Giggs of Manchester United.*

Mansell, Nigel (1954–)

English **motor-racing** driver. He started his **Formula 1** career with Lotus in 1980. Runner-up in the world championship on two occasions, he became world champion in 1992 and in the same year announced his retirement from Formula 1 racing, having won a British record of 30 Grand Prix races. He won the PPG Indycar series in the USA in 1993 before returning to Formula 1 racing in 1994.

Maracanã Stadium

The world's largest football stadium, in Rio de Janeiro, Brazil, built in 1950. It has a capacity of 175,000 but held a world record 199,854 spectators for the 1950 **World Cup** final between Brazil and Uruguay. It has also been used for world championship boxing contests and hosted the 1954 world basketball championship. A feature of the ground is the 2.25 m × 1.75 m/7 ft x 5 ft moat surrounding the pitch.

Maradona, Diego Armando (1960–)

Argentine **football** player. One of the outstanding players of the 1980s, he won over 80 international caps, and helped his country to three successive **World Cup** finals. He was South American footballer of the year 1979 and 1980. Despite his undoubted talent, his career was dogged by a series of drugs scandals, notably his disqualification from the 1994 World Cup after failing a drugs test. In the 1986 World Cup he appeared to use his hand illegally to score a winning goal against England – the infamous 'hand of God' incident.

marathon

Athletics endurance race over 42.195 km/26 miles 385 yd. It was first included in the **Olympic Games** in Athens in 1896. The distance varied until it was standardized in 1924. More recently, races have been opened to wider participation, including social runners as well as those competing at senior level. The marathon derives its name from the story of Pheidippides, a Greek soldier who ran the distance of approximately 39 km/24 mi from the battlefield of Marathon to Athens with the news of a Greek victory over the Persians in 490 BC. The current marathon distance was first used at the 1908 Olympic Games when the race was increased by an extra 385 yards from the 26 miles (the distance from Windsor to London) so that the race would finish in front of the Royal Box at the White City stadium.

Marciano, Rocky (Rocco Francis Marchegiano) (1923–1969)

US boxer, world heavyweight champion 1952–56. He retired after

49 professional fights, the only heavyweight champion to retire undefeated. Born in Brockton, Massachusetts, he was known as the 'Brockton Blockbuster'. He knocked out 43 of his 49 opponents. He was killed in a plane crash.

Marylebone Cricket Club (the MCC)

Founded in 1788 by a group of cricketing noblemen, the MCC was responsible for the growth of the game of cricket, drawing up and revising its laws until 1969, when lawmaking became the preserve of the International Cricket Council. English cricket is now run by the English Cricket Board. The MCC still owns Lord's Cricket Ground in London. Seen by many as a stuffy gentlemen's club with MCC members wearing 'egg and bacon' (yellow and red diagonal striped) ties, the club has been controversial, refusing to allow women to become members until 1999.

martial arts

Any of several styles of armed and unarmed combat developed in the East from ancient techniques and arts. Common martial arts include **aikido**, **judo**, **jujitsu**, **karate**, **kendo**, and **kung fu**.

Masters, the (golf)

The Masters was founded in 1934 by Bobby Jones, a great amateur golfer who won the grand slam in 1930. It is played every year on the Augusta National Golf Course and attracts the world's top golfers. Past winners have included Arnold **Palmer** (four wins), Jack **Nicklaus** (six), Gary **Player** (three), and Nick **Faldo** (three). In a link with the game's amateur traditions, in addition to the prize money, Masters' winners are also presented with a green jacket, which was awarded for the first time in 1949.

Mateo Flores Stadium tragedy

Tragedy during the qualifying rounds of the 1998 **World Cup** when 84 fans were killed at the Costa Rica–Guatemala **football** match, after supporters tried to get into the ground. The incident has been blamed on a combination of the sale of too many tickets sold officially and a glut of counterfeit tickets bringing too many fans into the Mateo Flores Stadium; it was estimated that almost 60,000 people had got into the 45,000-capacity stadium.

Matthews, Stanley (1915–2000)
English footballer who played for Stoke City, Blackpool, and England. He played nearly 700 Football League games, and won 54 international caps. He was the first Footballer of the Year in 1948 (and again in 1963), the first European Footballer of the Year in 1956, and the first footballer to be knighted for services to the game in 1965. An outstanding right-winger, he had the nickname 'the Wizard of the Dribble' because of his ball control. At the age of 38 he won an **FA Cup** Winners' medal when Blackpool beat Bolton Wanderers 4–3, Matthews laying on three goals in the last 20 minutes. He continued to play first-division football after the age of 50. At his death in 2000, the Football Writers' Association dedicated its annual Footballer of the Year award to his memory, calling it the Sir Stanley Matthews Trophy.

MCC
See *Marylebone Cricket Club.*

Melbourne Cup
Australian horse race, raced over 3.2 km/2 mi at Flemington Park, Victoria, on the first Tuesday in November. It was inaugurated in 1861.

Melrose RFC
Melrose RFC's main claim to fame is as the founders of sevens rugby (developed as a fund-raising idea). Success was fairly slow to come to the club after its formation in 1877, but since World War II, the border outfit has been one of Scotland's leading cubs, with six league titles, six Border League titles, and the SRU Cup three times. Melrose players include Craig Chalmers, Keith Robertson, and Jim Telfer.

Merckx, Eddy (1945–)

Belgian cyclist known as 'the Cannibal'. He won the **Tour de France** a joint record five times (1969–72 and 1974). Merckx turned professional in 1966 and won his first classic race, the Milan–San Remo, the same year.

> ❝I don't need dope, I win on the strength of my legs.❞
>
> **Eddie Merckx**, 1969.

Miami Dolphins

American football team formed in 1965. The Dolphins won two **Super Bowls** in their first 10 years and made the final of a third. Coached by Don Shula for 25 years, the Dolphins were lucky to have two of the game's great quarterbacks, Bob Griese and Dan Marino, leading their offence. Always in the top end of the AFC East conference, the Dolphins have won 200 of the 308 games they have played up to the end of the 1999–2000 season.

microlight flying

A microlight is a one-or two-seater aircraft with a maximum loaded weight of 390 kg/860 lb (though this may increase to 450 kg/992 lb), a fuel capacity of less than 50 litres and a wing loading of no more than 25 kg/m², and machines can reach speeds of 50–70 mph/80–113 kph. Microlight flying is regulated by the Civil Aviation Authority.

Millennium Stadium

Built partly with National Lottery funding as a replacement for **Cardiff Arms Park**, the 73,500-seater stadium was the centrepiece of the 1999 **Rugby World Cup.** In addition to rugby matches, it has also hosted Wales football matches and is expected to be the venue for the **FA Cup** while **Wembley** is being redeveloped.

Montana, Joe (1956–)

American football player who appeared in four winning **Super Bowls** as quarterback for the **San Francisco 49ers** in 1982, 1985,

1989, and 1990, winning the Most Valuable Player award in 1982, 1985, and 1990. He threw a record five touchdown passes in the 1990 Super Bowl. In January 2000, he was elected to the Pro Football Hall of Fame.

Monte Carlo Rally
Held every January in the tiny principality of Monaco, the Rally was first staged in 1911 and remains one of the key competitions in the World Rally Championship, thanks in particular to the myth of the 'last night' and the forcing of the Turini Pass which is more often than not snowed up. In 2001, the rally will be limited to 40 cars for the first time, forcing amateur drivers to take part in the Automobile club de Monaco's Historic Rally instead.

Montgomerie, Colin Stuart (1963–)
Scottish golfer who has won the Harry Vardon Trophy as the top-ranked player in the European Order of Merit a record seven times in succession, 1993–99. Success in the major tournaments eluded him, though he was runner-up in the **US Open** in 1994 and 1997, and the US **PGA** national championship in 1995. He has been a member of the Europe **Ryder Cup** side since 1991 and played a key role in the team's victories in 1995 and 1997. He played in the 1999 Ryder Cup in September 1999, and in October won the 1999 World Matchplay Championship. In May 2000, he won the prestigious Volvo PGA title at Wentworth, Surrey, for a record consecutive year.

Moore, Bobby (Robert Frederick) (1941–1993)
English footballer who led the England team to victory against West Germany in the 1966 World Cup final. A superb defender, he played 108 games for England 1962–70 (until 1978, a world-record number of international appearances) and was captain 90 times. His Football League career, spent at West Ham 1968–74 and Fulham 1974–77, spanned 19 years and 668 matches.

Moses, Ed(win Corley) (1955–)
US track athlete and 400-metre hurdler. Between 1977 and 1987 he

ran 122 races without defeat. He was Olympic champion in the 400-metre hurdles in 1976 and 1984 and World champion in the 400-metre hurdles in 1983 and 1987.

Moss, Stirling (1929–   )

English racing-car driver. Despite being one of the best-known names in British motor racing, Moss never won the world championship. He was runner-up on four occasions, losing to Juan Manuel **Fangio** in 1955, 1956, and 1957, and to fellow Briton Mike Hawthorn (1929–1959) in 1958. He received a knighthood in the 2000 New Year's Honours list.

> 6 There are two things no man will admit he can't do well, apparently: drive and make love. 9
> **Stirling Moss**, 1963.

motorcycle racing

Speed contests on motorcycles. It has many different forms:

- road racing over open roads
- circuit racing over purpose-built tracks
- speedway over oval-shaped dirt tracks
- motocross over natural terrain, incorporating hill climbs and
- trials, also over natural terrain, but with the addition of artificial hazards.

For finely tuned production machines, there exists a season-long world championship Grand Prix series with various categories for machines with engine sizes 125 cc–500 cc. Major events are the world championship, which has been in existence since 1949 (the **blue riband** event is the 500 cc class), and the **Isle of Man Tourist Trophy**, the principal race of which is the Senior TT.

motor racing

Competitive racing of motor vehicles. It has forms as diverse as hill-climbing, stock-car racing, rallying, sports-car racing, and **Formula 1** Grand Prix racing. The first organized race was from

❝ I think what it is really about is getting in a car and putting your foot down. ❞

James Hunt, British racing driver, 1976.

Paris to Rouen, France, in 1894. In Grand Prix racing (instituted 1906) a world championship for drivers has been in existence since 1950, and for constructors since 1958. The first six drivers and cars in each race are awarded points from ten to one; the cumulative

motor racing *German driver Michael Schumacher takes a curve in his Ferrari during the second day of free practice at the San Marino Grand Prix.*

total at the end of a season (normally 16 races) decides the winners. Other leading events apart from the world championship are the **Le Mans** Grand Prix d'Endurance, first held in 1923, and the Indianapolis 500, first held in 1911.

❝ I never say to anybody: 'See you next week.' ❞

Stirling Moss, British racing driver, 1965.

mountain biking

Recreational sport that enjoyed increasing popularity in the 1990s. Mountain bikes were developed from the rugged 'clunkers' ridden by a small group of off-road riders on the steep, rocky hillsides of Marin County, California in the mid-70s. The fashion spread and the first mass-produced model appeared in the USA 1981, and in the

UK in 1984. The first world championship was held in the USA in 1990 and has subsequently been held annually. National mountain-bike championships have been held in the USA since 1983 and in the UK since 1984. The sport was included as an Olympic event for the first time at Atlanta in 1996, with men's and women's cross-country races. Sometimes known as all-terrain bikes, or ATBs, mountain bikes have toughened frames with high ground clearance, wide tyres with a knobbly tread, wide, flat handlebars, powerful brakes (usually cantilevered), and a wide range of gears (typically 18 or 21).

mountaineering
Art and practice of mountain climbing. For major peaks of the Himalayas it was formerly thought necessary to have elaborate support from Sherpas (local people), fixed ropes, and oxygen at high altitudes (siege-style climbing). In the 1980s the Alpine style was introduced. This dispenses with these aids, and relies on human ability to adapt, Sherpa-style, to high altitude. In 1854 the Wetterhorn, Switzerland, was climbed by Alfred Wills, thereby founding the sport.

❝ Life is so simple on a mountain. ❞

Chris Bonnington, British mountaineer, 1978.

Munich air crash
Air disaster of February 1958, when **Manchester United's** youthful side (the so-called Busby babes) were flying back home after drawing the second leg of a European soccer competition against Red Star Belgrade. They refuelled at Munich but crashed on takeoff, killing 20 passengers; at a stroke the cream of English soccer was wiped out, including Duncan Edwards who was on the verge of greatness as a player. Survivors included manager Matt **Busby**, Bobby **Charlton**, and Harry Gregg. That the club rebuilt and came back in the next decade was a tribute to Busby's and the club's strengths.

Munich Olympics

Despite the exploits of Mark **Spitz** and Olga **Korbut**, the Munich games are best remembered for an attack by Palestinian terrorists acting with the Baader Meinhof terrorist group. The attack left 11 Israeli competitors, coaches, and officials dead.

Murrayfield

Scottish **rugby football** ground and home of the national team. It staged its first international in 1925 when Scotland beat England 14–11. The capacity is approximately 70,000. The ground was built on the site of the old Edinburgh Polo Ground at Murray's Field. The West Stand was added in the 1930s and the East Stand in the 1980s. Over 100,000 fans are reputed to have been in the ground for the match against Wales in 1975.

Navratilova, Martina (1956–)

Czech **tennis** player who became a naturalized US citizen in 1981. The most outstanding woman player of the 1980s, she had 55 **Grand Slam** victories by 1991, including 18 singles titles. She won the **Wimbledon** singles title a record nine times, including six in succession 1982–87. She was defeated by Conchita Martinez in the final of her last Wimbledon as a singles player in 1994. She became a tennis coach in February 1997, and made her debut as captain of the defending champion US **Fed Cup** team, replacing Billie Jean **King**.

Navratilova won her first Wimbledon title in 1976 (doubles with Chris **Evert**). Between 1974 and 1988 she won 52 Grand Slam titles (singles and doubles), second only to Margaret Court. Her first Grand Slam win was mixed doubles at the 1974 French Championship (with Ivan Molina of Columbia).

CAREER HIGHLIGHTS

Wimbledon
singles: 1978–79, 1982–87, 1990; doubles: 1976, 1979, 1981–84, 1986; mixed: 1985, 1993, 1995

US Open
singles: 1983–84, 1986–87; doubles: 1977–78, 1980, 1983–84

French Open
singles: 1982, 1984; doubles: 1975, 1982, 1984–88; mixed: 1974, 1985

Australian Open
singles: 1981, 1983, 1985; doubles: 1980, 1982–85

Nebiolo, Primo (1923–1999)

President of the **IAAF** for 18 years until his death, Nebiolo was, with Juan Antonio **Samaranch** and Avery **Brundage**, one of the legendary figures in the Olympic movement. His tenure as head of IAAF saw athletics become a big-money sport, and led to the rise of athletic superstars like Carl **Lewis** and Sergei **Bubka.** He was responsible for the staging of world indoor and outdoor championships, and campaigned for more money prizes to attract the biggest names.

netball

Game developed from **basketball**, played by two teams of seven players each on a hard court 30.5 m/100 ft long and 15.25 m/50 ft wide. At each end is a goal, consisting of a post 3.05 m/10 ft high, at the top of which is attached a circular hoop and net. The object of the game is to pass an inflated spherical ball through the opposing team's net. The ball is thrown from player to player; no contact is allowed between players, who must not run with the ball.

Newmarket

Town in Suffolk, eastern England, 21 km/13 mi northeast of Cambridge; a centre for horse racing since the reign of James I, it is the headquarters of the **Jockey Club** and the National Stud and site of the National Horseracing Museum (1983). There are two racecourses, the July course and the Rowley Mile Racecourse, both owned by the Jockey Club, and lying to the southwest. Approximately a fifth of the town's working population is employed in the racing industry, including veterinary services. The most important races held at Newmarket are the 1,000 and 2,000 Guineas, the Cambridgeshire, and the Cesarewitch.

New York Giants

American football team founded in 1925. Having had four different home grounds during their first 50 years, since 1976 they have played at the Giants Stadium. The Giants have won 17 NFL Divisional Championships and six NFL championships, including two Super Bowl championship titles. Famous players have included

Dallas Cowboys coach Tom Landry, TV commentator Frank Gifford, and Kyle Rote.

New York Mets
Baseball team founded in 1962 to bring National League baseball back to New York following the departure of the **New York Giants** and Brooklyn Dodgers in 1957. Playing at the historic Polo Grounds until 1964 and the Shea Stadium since, the New York Mets have won two **World Series**, three National League Pennants, and four Division Titles. Players have included Casey Stengel, Tom Seaver, and Nolan Ryan.

New York Yankees
Baseball team formed in 1901 that played under the name the 'Highlanders' until 1913. Playing at Hilltop Park until 1923, thereafter at their **Yankee Stadium**, the team has won 25 World Series titles, 36 American League Pennants, and eight division titles. 39 Yankee players are honoured in the Hall of fame, including **Babe Ruth**, **Joe DiMaggio**, Lou Gehrig, and Mickey Mantle.

Nicklaus, Jack William (1940–)
US golfer, nicknamed 'the Golden Bear'. He won a record 20 major titles, including 18 professional majors between 1962 and 1986. In 1999, the US magazine *Sports Illustrated* named him 'Best Individual Male Athlete of the 20th Century'.

Nike
Sporting goods company founded by Phil Knight in 1962. Once designing and manufacturing own-brand sports shoes, BRS changed its name to Nike and by 1979 the company dominated the industry, who by this time had branched into other sporting equipment. In 1972 the Nike 'tick' logo was introduced, depicting the wing of the Greek goddess, Nike. Nike have sponsored a multitude of sports teams and individuals, including **John McEnroe**, and **Michael Jordan**.

Norman, Greg (1955–   )
Australian golfer, nicknamed 'the Great White Shark'. After many wins in his home country, he enjoyed success on the European PGA Tour before joining the US Tour. He has won the World Match-Play title three times. He captained the International team to victory over the USA at Melbourne in the third President's Cup team competition in December 1998.

Nurmi, Paavo Johannes (1897–1973)
Finnish long distance runner. He was known as the 'Flying Finn', and won nine Olympic gold medals, including five at the 1924 Games. He broke 20 world records in 16 separate events ranging from the 1,500 metres to the 20,000 metres. Through his achievements and his scientific approach to training and racing he transformed competitive running in the 1920s. He set his first world record in 1921 in the 10,000 metres, and his last in 1931 when he became the first man to beat nine minutes in the two miles.

Oaks, the

Horse race, one of the English classics, run at Epsom racecourse in June, now run two days before the **Derby**, for three-year-old fillies only. The race is named after the Epsom home of the 12th Earl of Derby.

Oerter, Al (1936–   )

US **discus** thrower. One of the great Olympians, Al Oerter qualified for his first **Olympic Games** at the age of 19. Oertar's first throw won him the gold medal, and for the next three **Olympics** the first place on the rostrum was his. At Tokyo in 1964, he astonished the world by winning despite having dislocated a vertebra and turning up to the qualifying round in a neck brace. Retiring after his last gold medal, Oerter made a comeback and produced his best-ever throw of 69.46 m/221.89 ft in 1980 – 24 years after his first Olympic title.

officials in sport

'The men in the middle' are those required to enforce the laws, decide disputed calls, and in some cases dismiss violent or persistently infringing players. In track and field athletics, officials act as judges, measuring throws and jumps and timing races. In some of the more subjective events such as gymnastics or skating, the officials actually score performances.

Old Trafford

Two sporting centres in Manchester, England. Old Trafford **football** ground is the home of **Manchester United FC** and was opened in 1910. The record attendance was 76,692 at an FA Semi-final match in March 1939; the capacity was later reduced to 55,800, but increased to 61,000 following rebuilding in 2000, with an expected increase to 67,000 in 2001. Old Trafford **cricket** ground was opened in 1857 and has staged Test matches regularly since 1884 and is home to Lancashire County Cricket Club. The ground capacity is approximately 21,000.

Olympic Games

Sporting contests originally held in Olympia, ancient Greece, every four years during a sacred truce; records were kept from 776 BC. Women were forbidden to be present, and the male contestants were naked. The ancient Games were abolished in AD 394. The present-day games have been held every four years since 1896. Since 1924 there has been a separate winter Games programme; from 1994 the winter and summer Games are held two years apart.

Olympic Games, the ancient Games

Of all the many Games held in Ancient Greece, the Olympics were the oldest and most famous. Claims that certain mythical or even historical characters 'founded' the Olympic Games cannot be taken seriously. The Games were not suddenly established, but evolved from simple religious ceremonies to become the most grandiose sports festival of antiquity. Thus the origin of the Olympic Games is lost in obscurity, though evidence from excavations suggests that the sanctuary at Olympia dates from at least the 13th century BC. The first historical mention of the Games at Olympia dates from 776 BC, when a cook named Coroebus from Elis won the 'dromos', a sprint race one length of the stadium, and from this year also dates the four-year period or Olympiad – the interval at which the Games were held.

Olympic Games, the modern Games

The first modern Games were held in Athens, Greece. They were revived by Frenchman Pierre de Fredi, Baron de Coubertin (1863–1937), and have been held every four years with the exception of 1916, 1940, and 1944, when the two world wars intervened. Special tenth-anniversary Games were held in Athens in 1906. At the first revived Games, 245 competitors represented 14 nations in nine sports. At Atlanta in 1996, over 10,000 athletes represented 197 nations in 29 sports.

Olympic Games, events

The Games expanded over the centuries to include more varied events. In 724 BC the 'diaulos', two stadium lengths, was added; in 720 BC the 'dolichos' was added – 24 lengths of the arena (comparable to the modern 5,000 metre race). All of these races on foot were run up and down, not around, the arena. Boxing, chariot races, and the *pancratium* (a mixture of boxing and wrestling) were added in the 7th century BC, and at various times the following events were held at Olympia: pentathlon (long jump, discus, javelin, running, and wrestling), boys' events, and events for armed soldiers, heralds, and trumpeters. In addition to these sporting events, artists and sculptors exhibited their works and poets recited their poems. Not every event would be included at each celebration.

Olympics, Gay

The Gay Games were the brainchild of Tom Wadell, a decathlete in the 1968 US Olympic team. They were conceived as an opportunity to show that gay people share the same skills and competitive spirit as everyone else. In many ways it resembles Baron de Coubertin's Olympic ideal as the competition is less nationalistic, and greater emphasis is placed on doing one's personal best than winning.

Open, the (golf)

Britain's premier golf competition, the Open was first staged in 1860 and is played at various courses around the UK. The competition is based on 72 holes (four rounds) of stroke play, with the player with the lowest number of strokes winning. Entry is via a qualifying round, with some players exempted on the basis of their past performances.

Open, the Australian (tennis)

The Australian championships were first held in 1905, and are now run by Tennis Australia at Melbourne Park, Melbourne. The Open has men's and women's singles and doubles, mixed doubles, legend's doubles, legend's mixed doubles, and boys' and girls' singles and doubles.

Open, the French (tennis)
The French International Championship of tennis has been played since 1891, initially as a men's interclub competition at the Stade Français. Women were first admitted in 1897 and in 1925 the event was opened to non-French players. In 1928 the event was moved to the **Stade Roland Garros** and its clay courts, and in 1968 professional players were admitted.

Open, the US (golf)
A major golf tournament, the US Open is open both to amateurs and professional golfers, and has been held since 1895. Like the British **Open**, the competition is based on 72 holes (four rounds) of stroke play.

Open, the US (tennis)
The Open was first played in 1881 as a national men's singles and doubles event, and is now organised by the US Tennis Association and held at Flushing Meadow, NY at the USTA's National Tennis Centre. Women's competitions were added in 1887 (doubles in 190 and mixed doubles in 1892). Professionals were admitted to the Open in 1968.

orienteering
Sport of cross-country running and route-finding. Competitors set off at one-minute intervals and have to find their way, using map and compass, to various checkpoints (approximately 0.8 km/0.5 miles apart), where their control cards are marked. World championships have been held since 1966.

Ottey, Merlene (1960 –)
Jamaican athlete. Merlene Ottey has competed in six Olympic Games (1980–2000). In her first appearance, at the 1980 Moscow

Games, she became the first Jamaican woman to win an Olympic track and field medal when she took bronze in the 200 metres. She has won 14 World Championships medals – more than anyone in history. She withdrew from the 1999 World Championships after the result of a drug test taken at a July 1999 meeting in Switzerland came back positive for a banned steroid. In November 1999, a Jamaica Amateur Athletic Association panel cleared Ottey of charges of intentionally using performance-enhancing drugs, avoiding an automatic two-year suspension.

Ottey entered the 1992 Olympics nicknamed 'The Bronze Queen' because seven of her eight Olympic and World Championships medals up to that point were bronze. Appropriately, she finished third in the 200 metres in Barcelona. At the Atlanta Games, however, she won silver in the 100 metres and 200 metres. Ottey has become so revered in her native country that in 1993, after winning her first gold at the World Championships, she was named an ambassador of Jamaica. At the Sydney Olympic Games 2000 she came fourth in the 100-metre sprint and contributed to a 4 x 100-metre relay silver medal for the Jamaican team.

Oval, the
Cricket ground in Kennington, London, England, the home of Surrey County Cricket Club. In 1880 it was the venue for the first Test match to be held in England (between England and Australia).

Ovett, Steve (1955–)
British middle distance runner. There were many talented British runners during the 1970s and 1980s, but the rivalry between Sebastian **Coe** and Steve Ovett put both men head and shoulders above their rivals, and at one stage it seemed as if all middle distance records belonged to one or other of them. Their rivalry came to a head in the 1980 Moscow Olympics where Ovett ran a brilliant tactical race to steal the 800-metre from Coe, who came second in his favoured distance. Six days later it was Coe's turn to employ the best tactics in the 1,500 metres, with Ovett coming third, his first 1,500 metres defeat in three years. In 1983, Ovett set a world record

of 3 min 30.77 sec, but any hopes of capturing the Olympic 1,500-metre title were dashed when illness forced him to pull out of the 1984 final.

CAREER HIGHLIGHTS

Olympic Games
gold 800 metres 1980; bronze 1,500 metres 1980

European Championships
silver 800 metres 1974, 1978; gold 1,500 metres 1978

Commonwealth Games
gold 5,000 metres 1986

Owens, Jesse
(1913–1980)

The 1936 **Berlin Olympics** were meant to show how Germany under the Nazis was once more a world super-power. They became known as Jesse Owens' Olympics as Owens won four Olympic golds – the 100 metres in 10.3 secs, 200 metres in 20.7 secs, the long

Owens *Jesse Owens on his way to the 100 m gold medal, one of his four gold medals at the **Berlin Olympics**. Hitler refused to shake a black man's hand in congratulation.*

jump with 8.06 m/26.5 ft and leading off the 4 x 100-metres relay side that broke the world record. So angry was the Führer, that he refused to shake the winner's hand. Owens' greatness had been evident since 1935, when, at the Big 10 athletics championships at Ann Arbor, Owens set five world records and tied a sixth.

Palmer, Arnold Daniel (1929–)

US golfer who helped to popularize the professional sport in the USA in the 1950s and 1960s. He won **the Masters** in 1958, 1960, 1962, and 1964; the **US Open** in 1960; and the British **Open** in 1961 and 1962.

paragliding

Flying with the use of a foot-launched aerofoil canopy designed to be flown using the power of the wind, gravity, and the pilot's sheer strength. Similar to a steerable parachute, a paraglider is designed for soaring flight and not rapid descent. A pilot launches by running off gentle slopes and can rise to altitudes of 5,490 m/18,000 ft above sea level. Paragliding is a fast-growing sport in alpine regions.

Paralympic Games

An international sporting competition for athletes with disabilities, held every four years since 1948 in parallel with the **Olympic Games**. The Games were created by Dr Ludwig Guttmann, neurologist at Stoke Mandeville hospital in Buckinghamshire, England, as an extension of his rehabilitation programme for World War II veterans with spinal injuries. The first games, a competition between hospitals and sports clubs, took place at Stoke Mandeville on the opening day of the 1948 London Olympic Games, and thereafter they increased in size and scope. The 1988 games at Seoul were the first truly 'parallel' games, with several events taking place at the Olympic stadium, and also the first both to receive extensive media attention and to attract large crowds. At Sydney in 2000 3,824 athletes from 122 countries competed in sports ranging from **athletics**, **swimming**, **basketball**, and **archery**, to specially devised games such as **goalball** for the blind.

Parc des Princes

French sports stadium, until 1998 home of the national **rugby union** team. It has also staged international association football and was home to Paris's two senior football teams, Paris St Germain and Racing Club (disbanded in 1990). Parc des Princes can hold around 48,000 spectators. It staged the 1984 **European Championship** football final and was also used in the 1998 **World Cup** finals.

Pelé (1940–)

Adopted name of Edson Arantes do Nascimento, Brazilian soccer player. A prolific goal scorer, he appeared in four **World Cup** competitions 1958–70 and led Brazil to three championships (1958, 1962, 1970). In a poll conducted by the International Soccer Hall of Fame in 1997 he was voted the world's greatest footballer. Also in 1997 he received an honorary knighthood from Queen Elizabeth II of the UK.

pelota

Very fast ball game of Basque derivation, popular in Latin American countries and in the USA where it is a betting sport and is known as 'jai alai'. It is played by two, four, or six players, in a walled court, or *cancha*, and somewhat resembles squash, but each player uses a long, curved, wickerwork basket, or *cesta*, strapped to the hand, to hurl the ball, or pelota, against the walls.

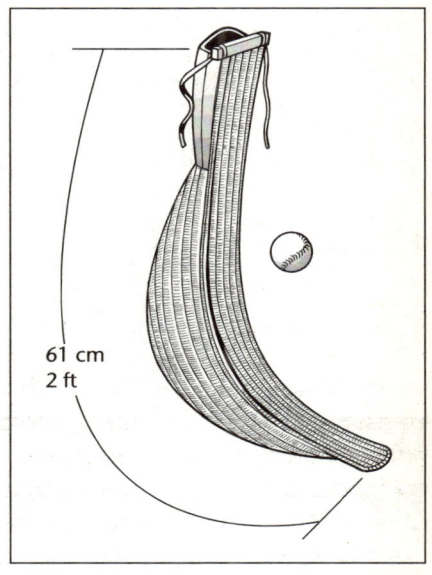

61 cm
2 ft

pelota *The* cesta *is a wicker basket made to a player's specifications. It has a chestnut frame, covered with woven reed. Front court players usually have smaller* cestas *than near court plars. The player's hand is inserted into a leather glove which is sewn to the outside of the* cesta. *A long tape is wrapped around the glove to keep it on the hand.*

pentathlon
Five-sport competition. Pentathlon consists of former military training pursuits: **swimming, fencing, running**, horsemanship, and **shooting**. It has been an Olympic event for men since 1912, but the Sydney 2000 Games were the first Olympics to include a women's event. The first modern pentathlon world championships for men took place in 1949, and for women in 1981.

Philadelphia Phillies
US **baseball** team. Formed in 1883, the Phillies are the oldest continuous, one-name/one-city franchise in all professional sports. Throughout their history they have played in four ballparks: Recreation Park (1883–87), National League Park (1887–1913), Baker Bowl (1913–38), and Veterans Stadium (1938–present day). A new stadium is in the pipeline for the team. The Phillies have won the **World Series** once, National League Championships five times, and Division Championships six times. Players have included Richie Ashburn, Mike Schmidt, Steve Carlton, and Robin Roberts.

pigeon racing
Sport of racing pigeons against a clock. The birds are taken from their lofts and transported to a starting point, often hundreds of miles away. They have to return to their loft and a special clock times their arrival. In the UK the National Homing Union dates from 1896. Elizabeth II has a flight of pigeons which is looked after by a racing manager.

Piggott, Lester Keith (1935–   )
English jockey. He adopted a unique high riding style and is renowned as a brilliant tactician. A champion jockey 11 times between 1960 and 1982, he rode a record nine **Derby** winners. Piggott retired from riding in 1985 and took up training. In 1987 he was imprisoned for tax evasion. He returned to racing in 1990 and has ridden 4,460 winners, including a record 30 classics to the start of the 1994 season. He retired as a jockey for the second time in September 1995.

Player, Gary Jim (1935–)

South African golfer who won major championships in three decades and the first British **Open** in 1959. A match-play specialist, he won the world title five times. His total of nine 'majors' is the fourth (equal) best of all time. He is renowned for wearing all-black outfits.

point-to-point

A form of horse racing over fences, organized by local hunts in the UK. It is open only to amateurs riding horses that have been regularly used in hunts. The point-to-point season lasts from January to May. Originally the races were between two points several miles apart and involved jumping natural obstacles, but in its modern form the course is circular and the fences are artificial.

poker

Card game of US origin, in which two to eight people play (usually for stakes) and try to obtain a 'hand' of five cards ranking higher than those of their opponents. The one with the highest scoring hand wins the 'pot' (the central pool). Standard kinds of poker are five-card draw and stud.

pole vault

Athletics field event in which the athlete attempts to clear a high cross bar by means of a long flexible pole. Competitive pole-vaulting for height as opposed to distance began in the mid-19th century. It has been an **Olympic** sport for men since the first modern games in 1896; however, women's pole vaulting was not treated seriously by the athletics authorities until the 1990s, and the Sydney 2000 Games were the first Olympics to include a women's as well as a men's pole vault event. Originally competitors used poles of ash, hickory, or spruce with a spike at the bottom. Bamboo poles were in use by the early 1900s, and were superseded by steel poles and then fibreglass.

polo

Stick-and-ball game played between two teams of four on horseback. It originated in Iran, spread to India and was first played in

England in 1869. Polo is played on the largest field of any game, measuring up to 274 m/ 300 yd × 182 m/ 200 yd. A small solid ball is struck with the side of a longhandled mallet through goals at each end of the

polo *A game of polo played in Germany in 1922.*

field. A typical match lasts about an hour, and is divided into 'chukkas' of $7\frac{1}{2}$ minutes each. No pony is expected to play more than two chukkas in the course of a day, as the game is exhausting for the animals. The rules of polo were evolved by the Hurlingham Club in 1875. Noted surviving British clubs are Cowdray Park, Sussex, and Roehampton, London, but the game is most popular in Argentina.

pool or pocket billiards
Game derived from **billiards** and played in many different forms. Originally popular in the USA, it is now also played in Europe. It is played with balls of different colours, each of which is numbered. The neutral ball (black) is the number eight ball. The most popular form of pool is eight-ball pool in which players have to sink all their own balls before the opponent, and then must sink the eight-ball to win the game. Other forms include sinking balls in numerical order (rotation), or sinking a designated ball into a designated pocket (straight pool).

Powderhall Sprint
A 110-metre race, now known as the New Year Sprint, which has been held since 1870 as part of the professional footracing traditions of Scottish sport. In past years the race has been held at Meadowbank Stadium, Edinburgh, and Musselburgh Racecourse.

powerboating

Racing with fast boats, with origins back as far as 1902 with the formation of the British Marine Motoring Association. The Union Internationale Motonautique (UIM), formerly Union Internationale de Yachting Automobile, founded in 1922, produced the first set of sporting rules and has remained the governing body of the sport. Powerboat racing is divided into 27 different UIM world championship classes depending on the complexity and power of the craft. Held in large indoor pools, Formula 1 is the prestigious category; its equivalent in offshore racing is the Class 1, which receives global media coverage.

powerlifting

The ultimate strength sport. It is distinct from **weightlifting** as it comprises three lifts: the squat, the bench press, and the deadlift. Powerlifting competitors are categorised by sex, age, and bodyweight. Each competitor is allowed three attempts at each lift, the best lift of each discipline being added to their total. Where a draw concludes a competition, the highest award is given to the competitor with the lowest bodyweight.

TYPES OF POWERLIFTS

Squat: The first and biggest of the three lifts. Standing upright with the barbell resting across the back of the shoulders, the lifter squats down to a required depth and then attempts to stand, resuming the original position.

Bench press: Lying flat on their back, the lifter holds the barbell at arms length above the chest. The bar is then lowered until it stops on the chest and then pushed ('pressed') back up again.

Deadlift: As the name implies, this is the lifting of a dead weight; with the barbell sitting on the floor, the lifter has to grip and lift the weight until they are standing upright with their shoulders back.

---

professionalism in sport

The amateur-professional debate helped shape the development of sports in this country. For example, though soccer went professional in the 19th century (as did **rugby league**), it was only at the end of the 20th century that **rugby union** and **athletics** went open (after years of what many termed 'shamateurism'). The Olympic ideal was competition for its own sake, with money being seen as tarnishing the process, as the witch-hunt that engulfed Jim **Thorpe** showed. In the UK, English **cricket** was one of the most rigidly class-bound sports, with 'gentlemen' (**amateurs**) and 'players' (the professionals) having separate dressing rooms, and the captaincy of England being reserved for the gentlemen until Len Hutton became the first professional captain. Purists would argue that although standards of fitness and skill have never been higher since the onset of fully professional team sports, the fact that the sport is now a 'job' has damaged sport by generating a safety-first attitude, with players reluctant to take risks: it is almost more important not to lose than to win well.

Prost, Alain Marie Pascal (1955–)

French **motor-racing** driver who was world champion in 1985, 1986, 1989, and 1993, and was the first French world drivers' champion. To the end of the 1993 season he had won 51 Grand Prix from 199 starts. He retired in 1993.

quadrathon
Sports event in which the competitors must swim 2 mi/3.2 km, walk 30 mi/48 km, cycle 100 mi/161 km, and 26.2 mi/42 km (a marathon) within 22 hours.

Queensberry, Marquess of (1844–1900)
British patron of **boxing**. In 1867 he gave his name to a new set of boxing rules. Devised by the pioneering British sports administrator John Chambers (1841–1883), the Queensberry Rules form the basis of today's boxing rules. He was the father of Lord Alfred Douglas and it was his misspelled insult to Oscar Wilde that set in motion the events leading to the playwright's imprisonment. He became marquess in 1858.

quoits
Game in which a rubber, rope, or metal ring (quoit) is thrown at a peg (hob) from a point 16.5 m/54 ft away. The player whose quoit lands nearest the hob, within a circle 1 m/3 ft in diameter, gains one point. A quoit that encircles the hob is called a ringer and is worth two points.

RAC Rally

Now known as the Rally of Great Britain, the first RAC Rally was held in 1932 over a course of 1,000 mi/1,609 km and used a similar format to the **Monte Carlo Rally**. By 1960, the course had increased to 2,000 m/3,219 km and included three timed stages on forest tracks for the first time. The event has remained virtually unchanged since that time, except that drivers are now allowed a pre-race reconnaissance on the spectator and special stages. It is part of the FIA World Rally Championship.

rackets or racquets

Indoor game played on an enclosed court. Although first played in the Middle Ages, rackets developed in the 18th century and was played against the walls of London buildings. It is considered the forerunner of many racket and ball games, particularly **squash**. The game is played on a court usually 18.3 m/60 ft long by 9.1 m/30 ft wide, by two or four persons each with a racket about 75 cm/2.5 ft long, weighing 255 g/9 oz. The ball is 25 mm/1 in in diameter and weighs 28 g/1 oz. Play begins from a service box – one is marked at each side of mid-court – and the ball must hit the end wall above a 2.75 m/9 ft high line. After service it may be played anywhere above a line 68.5 cm/27 in on the end wall, the general rules of tennis applying thereafter.

Ramsey, Alf(red Ernest) (1920–1999)

English **football** player and manager. England's most successful manager ever, he won the 1966 **World Cup**. Of the 113 matches in which he was in charge of the national side between 1963 and 1974, England had 69 victories, 27 draws, and only 17 defeats. He led England to the quarter-finals of the 1970 World Cup, but was sacked four years later after the team failed to qualify for the 1974 finals. As a player for Southampton and then **Tottenham**, he was capped 32 times by England.

Rangers FC

Rangers FC is the most successful **football** club in Scotland. The team first played as a founder member in the 1890–91 Scottish League season and has since won the Scottish League Championship 47 times, the Scottish Cup 27 times, the League Cup 20 times, and in the season of 1971–72 they won the European Cup Winners Cup. In their 101 seasons, Rangers FC have never been relegated. Based in Glasgow, their great rivals are **Celtic FC**.

Real Madrid FC

Leading Spanish **football** team. Founded in 1902, Real Madrid FC have won the Spanish First Division 27 times, UEFA Champions League seven times, the **UEFA Cup** twice, and the intercontinental Toyota Cup twice. The team play at the Bernabéu stadium, named after Santiago Bernabéu, the club president between 1943–75.

real tennis

Racket and ball game played in France, from about the 12th century, over a central net in an indoor court, but with a sloping roof let into each end and one side of the court, against which the ball may be hit. The term 'real' here means 'royal', not 'genuine'. Basic scoring is as for lawn tennis, but with various modifications. The oldest court still in use is the one installed by Henry VIII at Hampton Court, Richmond, London.

Redgrave, Steven Geoffrey (1962–   )

English oarsman, gold medallist at five successive Olympics, winning the coxed fours in 1984, the coxless pairs in 1988 and 1992, and the coxless fours in 1996 and 2000. He is the first man to win five Olympic golds at successive games in an endurance event. He also won nine gold medals at the World Championships 1986–99, a gold at the World Indoor Championships in 1991, and was a member of the winning four-man **bobsleigh** team at the national bobsleigh championships in 1989.

Red Rum

Racehorse whose exploits in the **Grand National** at **Aintree** won him national fame. The only horse to win the race three times, with victories in 1973, 1974, and 1977, he also finished second in 1975 and 1976. He died in 1995 at the age of 30, and is buried at Aintree near to the winning post.

Reebok

Sporting goods company, founded in Britain as Mercury Sports Ltd, which became Reebok Sports Ltd in the 1950s, and then Reebok International Limited. The company boomed in the 1980s, capitalizing on the growth of aerobics and the demand for shoes. Reebok now supplies shoes to athletes and shirts for the Welsh and Australian **rugby union** sides.

relay (athletics)

The relay race was first run in the USA, around 1880, to emulate the charity races organized by the New York fire service, where red pennants were handed on every 300 yards. The baton, a wooden cylinder 1 ft 30 in long, has now been replaced with a metallic version. The first relay events at an Olympic meeting took place in 1908. The races were divided into legs of 200 metres, 400 metres, and 800 metres, won by the US team with John Taylor becoming the first black athlete ever to win a gold medal. In the 1912 Olympics the 4 x 100-metre and 4 x 400-metre relays were introduced.

Rhiem, Karl-Hans (1941–)

West German **hammer** thrower. Karl-Hans Rhiem is remembered as one of the West's greatest hammer throwers at a time when Russian dominance of the sport was almost absolute, and it seemed only he could upset the Russian quartet of **Yuri Sedykh**, Igor Nikulin, Yuri Tann, and Sergei Litvinov. In a competition at Rehlingen, regarded as the best ever display in a field event, Rhiem threw all six of his hammers further than the previous world record, setting three new records in the process.

Richards, Viv (Isaac Vivian Alexander) (1952–)

West Indian cricketer. He was captain of the West Indies team 1986–91. He has played for the Leeward Islands and, in the UK, for Somerset and Glamorgan. A prolific run-scorer, he holds the record for the greatest number of runs made in Test cricket in one calendar year (1,710 runs in 1976). He retired from international cricket after the West Indies' tour of England in 1991 and from first-class cricket at the end of the 1993 season. In April 2000 he was voted the fifth greatest cricketer of the 20th century by the Wisden Cricketers' Almanack.

Rivaldo (1972–)

Rivaldo Victor Borba Ferreira, Brazilian **football** player who was voted the 1999 European and World footballer of the year. He made his international debut in 1993, but it was not until the 1998 **World Cup** finals, when he was one of the tournament's outstanding players, that he established his reputation as a world-class talent.

CAREER HIGHLIGHTS

International appearances
(1993–) 41; goals 19

South American Championship
1999

Spanish league championship
1998, 1999

Spanish Cup
1998

FIFA World Player of the Year
1999

European Footballer of the Year
1999

Robinson, Sugar Ray (1920–1989)

Adopted name of Walker Smith, US boxer. He was world welterweight champion 1945–51; he defended his title five times. Defeating Jake LaMotta in 1951, he took the middleweight title. He lost the title six times and won it seven times. He retired at the age of 45.

❝ Most people don't understand. I'm here to beat the other guy as bad as I can. He's got the same idea about me. Otherwise it's an exhibition. ❞

Sugar Ray Robinson, 1950.

rodeo
Originally a practical means of rounding up cattle in North America. It is now a professional sport in the USA and Canada. Ranching skills such as bronco busting, bull riding, steer wrestling, and calf roping are all rodeo events. Because rodeo livestock is valuable, rules for its handling are laid out by the American Humane Association. One of the most widely known rodeo shows is the Calgary Stampede in Alberta, Canada.

Rodnina, Irina Konstantinovna (1949–)
Soviet ice skater. Between 1969 and 1980 she won 23 World, Olympic, and European gold medals in pairs competitions. Her partners were Alexei Ulanov and then Alexsandr Zaitsev.

Ronaldo (1976–)
Born Luiz de Nazario de Lima Ronaldo, Brazilian **football** player who was voted FIFA World Player of the Year in 1996 and 1997. A prolific goalscorer, he has twice been transferred for world record fees, moving from PSV Eindhoven to **Barcelona** for £13.25 million in 1996, then a year later to **Inter Milan** for an estimated £21 million. He made his full international debut in 1994 and by October 1999 he had scored 36 goals in 53 internationals. He helped Brazil to win the 1999 South American Championship, the Copa America, staged in Paraguay.

roulette
Game of chance in which the players bet on a ball landing in the correct segment (numbered 0–36 and alternately coloured red or black) on a rotating wheel.

Bets can be made on a single number, double numbers, 3, 4, 6, 8, 12, or 24 numbers. Naturally the odds are reduced the more numbers are selected. Bets can also be made on the number being odd or even, between 1 and 18 or 19 and 36, or being red or black; the odds are even in each of those cases. The advantage is with the banker, however, because the 0 (zero) gives all stakes to the bank unless a player bets on 0. The play is under the control of a croupier.

rounders
Bat-and-ball game similar to **baseball** but played on a much smaller pitch. The first reference to rounders was in 1744.

rowing
Propulsion of a boat by oars, either by one rower with two oars (**sculling**) or by crews (two, four, or eight persons) with one oar each, often with a **coxswain**. Major events include the world championship, first held in 1962 for men and in 1974 for

rowers *British rowers Matthew Pinsent and Steven Redgrave in the Barcelona Olympics.*

women, and the **Boat Race** (between England's Oxford and Cambridge universities), first held in 1829. Rowing as a sport began with the English Leander Club in 1817, followed by the Castle Garden boat club, USA, in 1834.

royalty and sport
The British royal family have long been interested in sport. While many monarchs have been interested in **field sports** and latterly **tennis** and **horseracing** (the sport of kings), Henry VIII was a great archer and tennis player, and his active participation is reflected in today's crop of royals. While Princes Edward and Andrew play sport recreationally (in

golf and real tennis respectively), both Prince Charles and Princess Anne are competitive sportsmen. The Prince of Wales' love of **polo** is well-known and he played competitively; this love of the game has been inherited by Prince William. Princess Anne is a Montreal Olympic three-day event competitor, and a member of the **International Olympic Committee**. The Duke of Edinburgh is a **carriage-driver** of some talent. The queen's father, George VI played in the men's doubles at **Wimbledon** (while he was still Duke of York).

rugby league

Professional form of rugby football founded in England in 1895 as the Northern Union, when a dispute about pay caused northern clubs to break away from the Rugby Football Union. In Australia,

rugby league *A 1910 game of rugby league.*

the breakaway to semi-professional rugby occurred in a similar way. The first matches were played in 1907 against New Zealand and the New South Wales Rugby League was formed 1908. The game is similar to Rugby Union but the number of players was reduced from 15 to 13 and the scrum now plays a less important role as law changes have made the game more open and fast-moving.

rugby union

Form of rugby football, in which there are 15 players on each side. 'Tries' are scored by 'touching down' the ball beyond the goal-line or by kicking goals from penalties. The Rugby Football Union was formed in England in 1871 and has its headquarters at Twickenham, Middlesex. Formerly an amateur game, the game's status was revoked in August 1995 by the International Rugby Football Board and players could be paid for playing. It also lifted restrictions on players moving between rugby union and rugby league. It was announced in 1998 that rugby union (along with cricket) would be introduced to the Commonwealth Games for the first time at Kuala Lumpur, Malaysia, in September 1999. The Common-wealth tournament was played with seven players on each team, as opposed to the full 15-a-side version.

rugby union *Scotland versus Ireland in the Rugby Union World Cup.*

Women's rugby, started in 1983, is one of the fastest-growing women's sports.

❛This stone commemorates the exploit of William Webb Ellis who, with a fine disregard for the rules of football, as played in his time, first took the ball in his arms and ran with it, thus originating the distinctive feature of the rugby game. AD 1823.❜

Inscription on a marble tablet in Rugby school.

Rugby World Cup

First staged in 1987 in Australia and New Zealand, there have been four Rugby World Cups – all won by southern hemisphere teams (New Zealand in 1987, Australia in 1991, South Africa in 1995, and Australia again in 1999). England and France (twice) have both been runners up for the Webb Ellis Trophy, but the competition has emphasized the dominance of Australia, New Zealand, and South Africa. Australia and New Zealand will host the 2003 Cup. The 1999 World Cup was staged in the UK, and the final played at the **Millennium Stadium**, in Cardiff, Wales.

running

In sporting terms, running can be divided into categories: sprinting, middle distance, cross country, road running (**marathons, ultras**), **hurdles**, and **steeplechase**.

> ❝ I sometimes think that running has given me a glimpse of the greatest freedom that a man can ever know, because it results in the simultaneous liberation of both body and mind. ❞
>
> **Roger Bannister**, British runner, 1956.

TYPES OF RUNNING

sprinting: divided into 100 metres, 200 metres and 400 metres. The 100 metre sprint is the **blue riband** athletic event, offering the purest expression of human speed. Sprinting events started from a standing position until the introduction of **starting blocks** in 1937. Sprinting events are run in lanes.

middle distance: divided into races of various distances from 800 metres to 5,000 metres. These distances combine mental and physical strength with speed and analytical planning. They are raced on a stadium race circuit and are not run in lanes.

cross country: international competition began in 1898 between England and France. Cross country running combines endurance and mental strength, requiring power and grip to run through mud, water, snow, over barriers and up hills. Road runners often race cross country during the winter season to keep in shape.

road running: one of the main sporting activities in the 90s. Lengths of road races vary, the most popular being the **marathon** and half marathon.

Ruth, Babe (George Herman) (1895–1948)

US **baseball** player, regarded by many as the greatest of all time. He

CAREER HIGHLIGHTS

games
2,503

runs
2,174

home runs
714

average
.342

Word Series wins
1915–16, 1918, 1923, 1927–28, 1932

Ruth *Babe Ruth is regarded by many as the best baseball player of all time.*

was voted the best player in baseball history by editors of *The Sporting News* and, in December 1999 was named 'Best Baseball Player of the 20th Century' by US magazine *Sports Illustrated*. He played in ten **World Series**, and hit 714 home runs, a record that stood from 1935 to 1974 and led to the nickname 'Sultan of Swat'.

Ruth started playing baseball in 1914 as a pitch-outfielder for the Boston Braves before moving to the Boston Red Sox later that year. He joined the New York Yankees in 1920. He is the holder of the record for the most bases in a season: 457 in 1921. Yankee Stadium is known as 'the house that Ruth built' because of the money he brought into the club. A bat that he used in his last appearance at Yankee Stadium was bought by an unnamed collector for $107,000 during an auction in September 1999 in New York.

See also: *New York Yankees, Yankee Stadium.*

Ryder Cup

Golf tournament for professional men's teams from the USA and

Europe. It is played every two years, and the match is made up of a series of singles, foursomes, and fourballs played over three days. A women's version of the Ryder Cup, the Solheim Cup, was introduced in 1990. Named after entrepreneur Samuel Ryder, who donated the trophy in 1927, the tournament is played alternately in the USA and Europe.

Ryun, Jim (1947–)

James Ronald Ryun, US track athlete. In 1966 Ryun set a world record time of 3 min 51.3 sec for the mile. The next year he established a record for the 1,500 metres. He won a silver medal for the 1,500 metres in 1968, and turned professional after the 1972 Olympics. After suffering several injuries, he retired in 1976.

S

St Helens RLFC

The Saints were formed in 1873 as Eccleston Rangers and moved to Knowsley Road in 1890. The club played in the first **rugby league** Challenge Cup final but lost, but in the years since, Saints have brought many honours – the Challenge Cup (seven times), the Super league (twice), the championship (six times), and the Premiership Trophy (four times) are just the highlights. Great Saints include Kel Coslett, Mal Meninga, Scott Gibbs, and Bobby Goulding.

St Leger

Horse race held at Doncaster, England, every September. It is a flat race over 2,798 m/3,060 yd, and is the last classic of the season. First held in 1776, it is the oldest of the English classic races.

Samaranch, Juan Antonio (1920–   )

President of the **International Olympic Committee**. Samaranch, formerly a banker in Spain, is now the most powerful man in world sport. He became president in 1980 at a time of crisis; America was trying to muster a boycott of the 1980 Moscow Games and the IOC was struggling to generate funds. Now interest has never been greater, and the Olympics are enormously profitable, via sponsorships and television rights deals.

sambo

Sambo is a Russian military combat sport, literally meaning 'self defence without weapons'. The sport was created in the early 20th century by a serviceman, who developed a new kind of combat system from a mixture of western wrestling and oriental arts. Sambo wrestling is now an international sport, where competitions take place on a circular wrestling mat, with competitors wearing wrestling boots, Russian style shorts, and a tight fitting jacket called a kurta.

Sampras, Pete (1971–)

US **tennis** player. At the age of 19 years and 28 days, he became the youngest winner of the US Open in 1990. A fine server and volleyer, Sampras also won the inaugural Grand Slam Cup in Munich in 1990. In 1997 he finished at the top of the ATP men's world rankings for an unprecendented fifth consecutive year. In August 1999 he beat Ivan Lendl's all-time record of 270 weeks at the top of the ATP Tour world rankings.

> **CAREER HIGHLIGHTS**
>
> *Wimbledon*
> singles: 1993–95, 1997–2000
>
> *Australian Open*
> singles: 1994, 1997
>
> *US Open*
> singles: 1990, 1993, 1995–96
>
> *Grand Slam Cup*
> 1990
>
> *ATP Tour World Championship*
> 1991, 1994, 1996, 1997

In 2000 he won his seventh Wimbledon men's singles title, equalling the record established by English player William Renshaw between 1882 and 1889. It was Sampras's 13th Grand Slam singles title, an unprecedented achievement in the men's game.

Sanderson, Tessa (Theresa Ione) (1956–)

English sportswoman and television presenter. Having first thrown the **javelin** for Great Britain in 1974, she kept the country at the top of the event throughout her competitive career, along with her great rival Fatima **Whitbread**. Though later dogged by injury, she won three Commonwealth gold medals (1978, 1986, and 1990), and one Olympic gold medal at the Los Angeles games in 1984. In 1989 she became a sports newsreader for Sky TV.

San Francisco 49ers

American football team founded in 1946. They were a founding member of the All-American Conference and upon its dissolution they joined the National League in 1950. One of the leading teams of the 1980s, they have won five **Super Bowl** championships and players have included Joe Perry, Hugh McElhenny, and John Brodie.

Santa Monica Track Club

Founded in 1972 by Joe Douglas, the Santa Monica Track Club became famous through its athlete members, sprinters Carl **Lewis** and Evelyn Ashford and middle distance runner Johnny Grey. Club members have won 27 Olympic medals, 17 of them gold, and 18 world championships.

scandals in sport

While there is always a danger that individuals will cheat, either by breaking the rules or taking performance-enhancing drugs of their own volition, occasionally such organized, premeditated cheating occurs, sometimes involving a conspiracy, that scandal ensues. Some scandals are related to betting coups, for example the attempt to rig the 1919 World Series by Hyman Roth, or former South African **cricket** captain Hansie Cronje's admissions that he took money from bookmakers. Others, only now coming to light as the old Eastern Bloc opens up, suggest state collusion over athletes' steroid abuse (in some cases reports suggest athletes were given steroids without their knowledge). The 1987 World Athletics Championships at Rome were tarnished after it was discovered that the long jump was rigged by officials to give a bronze medal to an Italian jumper.

sculling

Sculling is the rowing technique of using two oars in unison, as opposed to a single oar per rower. Events include single and double (two oarsmen) sculls.

Sedykh, Yuri (1955–   )

One of the greatest Russian **hammer** throwers who, with Yuri Tann, Sergei Litvinov, and Igor Nikulin, dominated the ball and chain event in the 1970s and 1980s. His world record of 86.74 m/284.58

ft (set in 1986) has not been bettered. He struck Olympic gold in 1976 and 1980, and might have added a third but for Russia's boycott of the Los Angeles Games in 1984. He was world champion in 1981.

seeding

The selecting of teams or competitors as seeds, depending on their past performance in an particular competition and/or current form, is often carried out to ensure that one half of a draw is not top-heavy with the better competitors, and the seeds are then distributed throughout the tournament. If seeding has been carried out efficiently, in an ideal environment the two top seeds would play in the final, but the uncertainty of sport and the way athletes rise to the big occasions means that this may not happen.

Senna, Ayrton (1960–1994)

Brazilian **motor-racing** driver. He won his first Grand Prix in Portugal in 1985 and won 41 Grand Prix in 161 starts, including a record six wins at Monaco. Senna was world champion in 1988, 1990, and 1991. He was killed at the 1994 San Marino Grand Prix at Imola.

sex tests, Olympic

Since 1968, the International Olympic Committee has required all individuals to provide genetic evidence of their femininity, two years after athletes were first required to undergo sex testing. The situation arose because of concerns that some female athletes were in fact male or intersexual (hermaphrodites), with Czech 800 metres runner Zdenka Koubkowa breaking the world record in 1934 only to be subsequently diagnosed as a hermaphrodite. The first athlete to fail a sex test was Polish runner Eva Klobukskowa who, despite passing the old style physical examination, was found to have an extra male chromosome, and was banned from competition. (In retirement she became pregnant and gave birth to a healthy child!) It may have been coincidence but a number of athletes, mainly heavy throws athletes from the Eastern Bloc countries, retired as soon as sex testing was first introduced. It is understood the only female Olympic competitor not required to have to produce evidence of femininity since 1968 was Princess Anne.

STELLA WALSH

In 1936, the US athlete Helen Stephens was accused of being a man after beating Polish sprinter Stanisllawa Walsiewicz (Stella Walsh). Stephens was confirmed to be a woman but when Stella Walsh was shot dead as an innocent bystander in a robbery in Cleveland, during an autopsy she was found to have male genitalia. Whether she was an intersexual or had deliberately pretended to be a woman to achieve sporting honours, will never be known.

Sheene, Barry Stephen Frank (1950–)

English motorcycle racer. He won the British 125cc title in 1970, and gave Suzuki their first victory by gaining the 500cc world championship in 1976, winning it again in 1977, and being runner-up in 1978. He holds the fastest-ever average speed for a world championship race (217.37 kmh/135.07 mph). In 1981 he raced for Yamaha but, after a crash at Silverstone in 1982, he retired to pursue a career in broadcasting in Australia.

shinty

Gaelic *camanachd*, stick-and-ball game resembling **hurling**, popular in the Scottish Highlands. It is played between teams of 12 players each, on a field 132–183 m/144–200 yd long and 64–91 m/70–99 yd wide. A curved stick (*caman*) is used to propel a leather-covered cork and worsted ball into the opposing team's goal (*hail*). The premier tournament, the Camanachd Cup, was instituted in 1896.

Shoemaker, Willie (William Lee) (1931–)

US jockey 1949–90. He rode 8,833 winners from 40,351 mounts and his earnings exceeded $123 million. He retired in February 1990 after finishing fourth on Patchy Groundfog at Santa Anita, California.

shogi

Japanese board game. It probably derives from the same Indian sources as **chess**, but is more complex. There are 20 million shogi players in Japan (1996). Yoshiharu Habu, a 25-year-old grand master, won all seven main shogi championships in February 1996, and has become a national hero in Japan.

shooting

Shooting can be divided into two disciplines, clay pigeon and target.

TYPES OF SHOOTING

Clay pigeon: The art of shooting at special flying targets, known as clay pigeons or clay targets, with a shotgun.
Target: Using air rifles and pistols to hit specified targets. Although pistol shooting is an Olympic shooting discipline, UK competitors face training difficulties since it became illegal to possess such firearms in 1997.

shooting *Clay pigeon shooting.*

short tennis

A variation of lawn **tennis**. It is played on a smaller court, largely by children. It can be played indoors or outdoors.

shot put or putting the shot

In athletics, the sport of throwing (or putting) overhand from the shoulder a metal ball (or shot). Standard shot weights are 7.26 kg/16 lb for men and 4 kg/8.8 lb for women.

Silverstone
Britain's oldest **motor-racing** circuit, opened on 2 October 1948. It is situated near Towcester, Northamptonshire, and was built on a disused airfield after World War II. It staged the first officially-titled British Grand Prix in 1948 and on 13 May 1950 hosted the inaugural Grand Prix of the **Formula 1** World Drivers' Championship. In 1987 it became the permanent home of the British Grand Prix.

Six Nations, the
Domestic European **rugby union** tournament contested every year by France, Italy, England, Scotland, Ireland, and Wales. The Six Nations' games are played in the second half of the season.

skateboarding
Single flexible board mounted on wheels and steerable by weight positioning. As a land alternative to surfing, skateboards developed in California in the 1960s and became a worldwide craze in the 1970s. Skateboarding is practised in urban environments and has enjoyed a revival since the late 1980s.

skating
Self-propulsion on ice by means of bladed skates, or on other surfaces by skates with small rollers (wheels of wood, metal, or plastic). The chief competitive ice-skating events are figure skating, for singles or pairs, ice-dancing, and simple speed skating. The first world ice-skating championships were held in 1896. Ice-skating became possible as a world sport from the opening of the first artificial ice rink in London, England, 1876. The roller skate was the invention of James L Plympton, who opened the first rink in Newport, Rhode Island, USA in 1866;

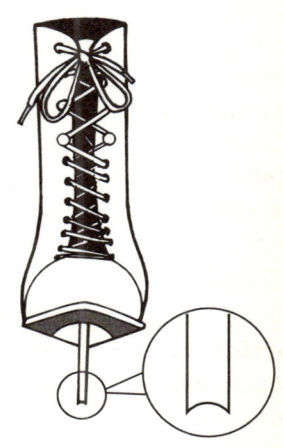

skating *Skates usually have a single steel blade about 3mm wide. The blade is hollow-ground on the bottom to give two skating edges, figures are skated on the inside or the outside edge.*

events are as for ice-skating with European and world championships.

skiing

Self-propulsion on snow by means of elongated runners (skis) for the feet, slightly bent upward at the tip. It is a popular recreational sport, as cross-country ski touring or as downhill runs on mountain trails; events include downhill; slalom, in which a series of turns between flags have to be negotiated; cross-country racing; and ski jumping, when jumps of over 150 m/490 ft are achieved from ramps up to 90 m/295 ft high. Speed-skiing uses skis approximately one-third longer and wider than normal with which speeds of up to 200 kph/125 mph have been recorded. Recently, **snowboarding** (or monoboarding), the use of a single, very broad ski, similar to a surf board, used with the feet facing the front and placed together, has become increasingly popular.

skittles or ninepins

Game in which nine wooden pins, arranged in a diamond-shaped frame at the end of an alley, are knocked down in three rolls from the other end of the alley with a wooden ball. Two or more players can compete. Skittles resembles tenpin bowling. A smaller version called table skittles is played indoors on a table using a pivoted ball attached to a pole by a chain.

skydiving or parachuting

Sport of freefalling from an aircraft at a height of up to 3,650 m/12,000 ft, performing aerobatics, and opening a parachute when 600 m/2,000 ft from the ground. The first ever parachute jump was made by André-Jaques Garnerin in 1797, using a basket under an open parachute made of silk and stiffened with supporting poles. The limp parachutes that are used today for skydiving were not developed until 1897. American Leslie Irvin made the first ever international free-fall parachute jump in 1919 using his own hand-operated chute, from which the new sport was born. The first World Championships were held in 1951 and have been held every two years since. The sport has developed to include extreme events, such as skyboarding, where the parachutist 'surfs' whilst freefalling using the board attached to the feet.

snooker
Indoor game derived from **billiards** (via **pool**). It is played with 22 balls: 15 red, one each of yellow, green, brown, blue, pink, and black, and one white cueball. A tapered pole (cue) is used to move the balls across the table. Red balls are worth one point when sunk, while the coloured balls have ascending values from two points for the yellow to seven points for the black. The world professional championship was first held in 1927. The world amateur championship was first held in 1963. A snooker World Cup team event was inaugurated at Bangkok, Thailand, in 1996. The **International Olympic Committee** recognized snooker as an Olympic sport in 1998; snooker is likely to make its Olympic debut at the Athens games in 2004.

snowboarding
First invented in 1929, snowboarding is a growing sport in alpine regions. Based on a surfboard design, modern snowboards are made of fibreglass. The first international snowboard race took place in the USA in 1982 and freestyle events are now commonplace. The sport was represented for the first time at the 1998 Nagano **Winter Olympics**, where two disciplines were contested: downhill slalom and the half pipe (freestyle).

Sobers, Garry (Garfield St Auburn) (1936–)
West Indian Test **cricketer**, arguably the world's finest ever all-rounder. He held the world individual record for the highest Test innings with 365 not out, until beaten by Brian Lara in 1994. He played **county cricket** for Nottinghamshire and, in a match against Glamorgan at Swansea in 1968, he became the first to score six sixes in an over in first-class cricket. He played for the West Indies on 93 occasions, and was captain 39 times. He was knighted in 1975.

softball
Bat and ball game, a form of **baseball** played with similar equipment. The two main differences are the distances between the bases (18.3 m/60 ft) and that the ball is pitched underhand in softball. There are two forms of the game, fast pitch and slow pitch; in the latter the ball must be delivered to home plate in an arc that must not be less than 2.4 m/8 ft at its height. The fast-pitch world championship was instituted in 1965 for women and in 1966 for men; it is now contested every four years.

Spartakiad
Sports games held every four years in the former USSR (so named from ancient Sparta's stress on physical fitness for state service), in which about 10,000 Soviet athletes compete (foreigners were admitted from 1979).

speedskating
The sport of speedskating is derived from its practical value; like cycling and running, people speedskated each day as a means of getting from place to place. The first all-iron skates were developed in Scotland in 1572, moving speedskating into the realms of an organized sport. The first speedskating competition is thought to be a 15-mile race held on the Fens in England in 1763. The first club was established in the USA in 1849 and the first official race took place in Oslo in 1863. 1924 saw the inclusion of speedskating in the Winter Olympics in Chamonix, France.

Spitz, Mark (1950–   )
US swimmer. At the 1972 **Munich Olympics**, he won a record seven gold medals and established many world records. During the games he

6 My moustache also helps my swimming. It catches the water and keeps it out of my mouth. 9

Mark Spitz, 1972.

had security protection as 11 Israeli athletes had been murdered by terrorists and it was feared that he himself might have been a target because of his Jewish faith.

sponsorship
Form of advertising in sports, music, broadcasting, and the arts. Sponsorship became a major source of finance for sport in the 1970s, and takes several forms. Many companies sponsor sporting events, while others pay money to individuals who wear the company's logo or motifs on their kit while performing.

Springboks, the
Nickname for the South African rugby side, taken from the emblem on their shirts. South Africa first wore green shirts in 1896 and in 1903 won their first series: it was not until 1953 that they lost another one. When South Africa toured Britain in 1906, they had a shirt badge made, the first time South Africans wore the Springbok. After 1953, the Boks were never as dominant, and once sanctions kicked in over apartheid, they were starved of serious international competition. Once South Africa liberalized and Nelson Mandela was freed, the Springbok revival was completed when South Africa won the 1995 **Rugby World Cup**. Great players include Freek du Preez, Morne du Plessis, Naas Botha, and Francois Pienaar, but the greatest figure in Springbok rugby is administrator Danie Craven.

squash or squash rackets
Racket-and-ball game usually played by two people on an enclosed court, derived from rackets. Squash became a popular sport in the 1970s and later gained competitive status. There are two forms of squash: the American form, which is played in North and some South American countries, and the English, which is played mainly in Europe and Commonwealth countries such as Pakistan, Australia, and New Zealand. Squash was first played at Harrow public school in 1817. The Squash Rackets Association was formed in 1928. The World Open championship was first held in 1975.

Stade de France

French sports stadium built to host the France 98 football **World Cup**. Situated a few miles north of Paris, in Saint-Denis, the Stade de France seats 80,000 spectators.

Stade Roland Garros

French lawn-tennis centre at Auteil, Paris, built in the 1920s for the French team to play their matches in defence of the **Davis Cup**. It became the home of the **French Open** Championships 1928.

Stanley Cup

North American **ice hockey** playoffs held at the end of the regular season in the National Hockey League (NHL). The Stanley Cup was donated in 1893 by Lord Stanley of Preston, the Governor General of Canada 1888–93, as a challenge cup to be presented to the 'leading hockey club in Canada' (this was intended to mean leading amateur club). In 1914, however, it was awarded to the winner of a playoff between the winners of Canada main professional leagues – the eastern National Hockey Association (NHA) and the western Pacific Coast Hockey Association (PCHA). The NHA was disbanded in 1917 and replaced by the newly formed national Hockey League (NHL) whose first season ran 1917–18. In 1923 and 1924 the winners of the Western Canada Hockey League (WCHL) also competed for the cup. In 1924 the PCHA was disbanded. In the 1925–26 season the ECHL became the Western Hockey League after which it, too, was disbanded. Since 1927 the Stanley Cup has been awarded exclusively to the winner of the National Hockey League (NHL) playoffs.

starting blocks (athletics)

Starting blocks have officially been used at the start of sprint races since 1937. Prior to this, athletes dug footholds into the cinder track to gain grip. Starting blocks have evolved to include pressure pads to monitor the athletes' movement, preventing anyone getting an unfair advantage from beating the gun. Starting blocks also provide athletes with a surface from which they can push off at the start of the race, giving them acceleration from the first step.

steeplechase (athletics)

This event was born out of a wager among Oxford University students in 1850, imitating horseracing. Initially held over two miles, early steeplechases were cross-country, crossing hurdles, streams, and other obstacles. It entered the 1900 **Olympic Games** as a track event, where it was run on an arena track. Runners are required to jump a hurdle and water jump once each lap. The current standard steeplechase distances are 2,000 metres and 3,000 metres and Kenya have won every Olympic Games steeplechase gold medal since 1984.

Stewart, Jackie (John Young) (1939–   )

Scottish motor-racing driver. Until surpassed by Alain **Prost** (France) in 1987, Stewart held the record for the most **Formula 1** Grand Prix wins (27). He entered a Formula 1 team in partnership with his son Paul for the 1997 and 1998 championships.

His first win was in 1965, and he started in 99 races. With manufacturer Ken Tyrrell, Stewart built up one of the sport's great partnerships. His last race was the 1973 Canadian Grand Prix. He pulled out of the next race (which would have been his 100th) because of the death of his team-mate Francois Cevert. He has also worked as a motor-racing commentator.

stock-car racing

Sport popular in the UK and the USA, but in two different forms. In the UK, the cars are 'old bangers', which attempt to force the other cars off the track or to come to a standstill. This format is known in the USA as 'demolition derbies'. In the USA, stock cars are high-powered sports cars that race on purpose-built tracks at distances up to 640–800 km/400–500 mi.

stoolball

Ancient game, considered the ancestor of **cricket**, the main differences being that in stoolball bowling is underarm, the ball is soft, and the bat is wooden and shaped like a tennis racket.

sumo wrestling

National sport of Japan. Fighters of larger than average size (rarely less than 130 kg/21 st or 285 lb) try to push, pull, or throw each other out of a circular ring. Fighters follow a traditional diet and eat a great deal to build up body weight. In the ring, they try to get their centre of gravity as low to the ground as possible. Championships, lasting up to 15 days each, are held six times a year in Japan; millions of fans watch the contests live and on television. Sumo wrestling originated as a religious ritual performed at Shinto shrines. In the 17th and 18th centuries it evolved into a popular spectator sport.

Super Bowl

US professional football championship, inaugurated in 1966. It is the annual end-of-season contest between the American Football Conference (AFC) and the National Football Conference (NFC) champions. **See also:** *American football.*

surfing

Sport of swimming in the surf and of riding waves towards the shore, either while standing on a narrow, keeled surfboard, or while lying on one of a variety of other shorter boards, or by holding the body stiff, as if it were a board, and allowing oneself to be carried along by the force of the water. The last is also known as body-surfing. Surfboard riding developed in Hawaii and Australia. The board is usually of light, synthetic material, about 1.8 m/5 ft long. The first properly organized world champi-

surfing *A surfer at La Jolla Beach, California, USA.*

onship was held at Manly, New South Wales, in 1964, although other competitions had previously been considered the world championships.

> 6 When that big, hollow, motherless wave comes crashing down behind you, and it vibrates the whole ocean and you come out of it alive, and you're so stoked you can't stand it, it is being unplugged from life for just a second. God, it's the neatest thing. 9
>
> **Phil Edwards**, US surfer.

Swansea RFC
Set up as a football club in 1872, 'the Jacks' switched to rugby in 1874 and play at St Helens sports ground, Swansea. League champions and winners of the WRU Cup three times each, Swansea have produced a host of great players including Mervyn Davies, Scott Gibbs, and Robert Jones.

swimming
There are four strokes in competitive swimming: freestyle, breaststroke, backstroke, and butterfly. Distances of races vary between 50 metres and 1,500 metres. Olympic-size pools are 50 m/55 yd long and have eight lanes. Special types of swimming include **synchronized swimming**, a form of 'ballet' performed in and under water. Underwater swimming developed with the invention of such equipment as flippers, snorkel, and self-contained underwater breathing apparatus (scuba). A related sport is **diving**. Swimming has been included in the **Olympic Games** since 1896 for men and since 1912 for women.

swimming, synchronized
Swimming discipline that demands artistry as opposed to speed. Competitors, either individual (solo) or in pairs, perform rhythmic

routines to music, which include difficult but graceful movements called 'stunts,' similar to diving positions. Points are awarded for interpretation, style, and stunt performance (multiplied by a degree of difficulty scale as in diving). It was introduced into the Olympic swimming programme in 1984.

table tennis or ping pong

Indoor game played on a rectangular table by two or four players. It was developed in Britain about 1880 and derived from lawn tennis. The world championships were first held in 1926. Play takes place on a table measuring 2.74 m/9 ft long by 1.52 m/5 ft wide. Across the middle is a 15.25 cm/6 in high net over which the ball must be hit. The players use small, wooden paddles covered in sponge or rubber.

tae kwon do

Korean martial art similar to karate, which includes punching and kicking. It was included in the 1988 **Olympic Games** as a demonstration sport, and became a full medal discipline at the Sydney 2000 Olympic Games.

Tailteann Games

Early 20th-century revival of an ancient festival held at Teltown, County Meath, Republic of Ireland. Originally presided over by the Uí Néill kings of Tara, the festival observed the advent of winter and was held from 632 BC until 1169. A historical and political symbol of the kingship of Tara, the festival was promoted by both Brian Bóruma and Rory O'Connor in recognition of their high kingship of Ireland. Then, having lapsed for 755 years, the festival was revived in 1924 as the 'Tailteann Games' with a gathering of international athletes at Croke Park. Held again in 1928 and 1932 as 'Aonach Tailteann' or 'the festival of Teltown', the event consisted of several athletic competitions, with games of hurling and Gaelic football as highlights. After the suspension of the games in 1932, they resumed again in 1963 and are now staged as a festival of schools athletics each summer.

Tattersall's

British auctioneers of racehorses based at Knightsbridge Green, southwest London, since 1864. The firm is named after Richard Tattersall (1724–1795), who founded Tattersall's at Hyde Park Corner in 1766.

tennis

Racket-and-ball game invented towards the end of the 19th century. Although played on different surfaces (grass, wood, shale, clay, concrete), it is also called 'lawn tennis'. The aim of the two or four players (in singles or doubles matches) is to strike the ball into the prescribed area of the court, using oval-headed rackets (strung with gut or nylon), in such a way that it cannot be returned. The game is won by those first winning four points (called 15, 30, 40, game), unless both sides reach 40 (deuce), when two consecutive points are needed to win. A set is won by winning six games with a margin of two over the opponents, though a tie-break system operates at six games to each side (or in some cases eight) except in the final set. A match lasts a maximum of five sets for men and three for women. Major events include the **Davis Cup**, first contested in 1900, and the annual All England Tennis Club championships (originating in 1877), an open event for players of both sexes at **Wimbledon**. Wimbledon is one of the four **Grand Slam** events; the others are the US Open (see **Open, the US**); the French Championships; and the Australian Championships.

> Tennis was introduced by Major Walter Clopton Wingfield at a Christmas party at Nantclwyn, Wales, in 1873. His game was then called 'Sphairistike'. It derived from **real tennis**, which was played in France from about the 12th century.

❛ Tennis is a game of inches. ❜

Jimmy Connors, US tennis star, 1975, on losing Wimbledon to Arthur Ashe.

Test match
Sporting contest between two nations, the most familiar being those played between the nine nations that play Test cricket (England, Australia, West Indies, India, New Zealand, Pakistan, South Africa, Sri Lanka, and Zimbabwe). Test matches can also be found in Rugby League and Rugby Union.

Thompson, Daley Francis Morgan (1958–)
English decathlete who broke the world record four times since winning the **Commonwealth Games** decathlon title in 1978. He won two more Commonwealth titles (1982, 1986), two **Olympic** gold medals (1980, 1984), three European medals (silver 1978; gold 1982, 1986), and a world title (1983). He retired in 1992.

thoroughbred
Horse bred for racing purposes. All racehorses are thoroughbreds, and all are direct descendants of one of three stallions imported into Britain during the 17th and 18th centuries: the Darley Arabian, Byerley Turk, and Godolphin Barb.

Thorpe, Ian (1982–)
Australian swimmer. Known as the 'Great Thorpedo' he shaved nearly two seconds off the 400-metre freestyle world record at the 1999 Pan Pacific Championships and then claimed the world record for the 200-metre freestyle event.

During the build-up to the Sydney Olympic Games 2000 he improved on both world records and was the presumptive favourite to win gold in the 200-metre and 400-metre freestyle events. He won the gold medal in the 400-metre freestyle event in yet another world record time, gold again in the 4 x 100-metre freestyle relay, silver in the 200-metre freestyle, and was the anchorman in the 4 x 400-metre freestyle relay team that took gold in a world record time.

Thorpe, Jim (James Francis) (1888–1953)
US athlete. A member of the 1912 US Olympic Team in Stockholm, he won gold medals for the **decathlon** and **pentathlon**. He was

forced to return the medals when he admitted that he had played semi-professional baseball. He played major-league **baseball** 1913–19 and was an outstanding player of professional football 1917–29. His Olympic medals were restored to him by the Amateur Athletic Union in 1973.

toboggan

Flat-bottomed sledge, curved upwards and backwards at the front, used on snow or ice slopes or banked artificial courses. An example of such a course is the Cresta Run in Switzerland. Olympic toboggans are either luge type seating one or two, without brakes or steering; or bobsleighs seating two or four, with streamlined 'cowls' at the front, steering, and brakes. A skibob is like a bicycle with skis replacing the wheels, and the rider wears miniature foot skis up to 50 cm/20 in long.

Toronto Blue Jays

Major League **baseball** team. Founded in 1977 and playing initially at Exhibition Stadium and then at the Sky Dome. The Toronto Blue Jays have won the American League East Championship five times, the American League Championship twice, and the **World Series** twice.

Torvill and Dean

Jayne Torvill (1957–) and Christopher Dean (1959–), English ice-dance champions. They won the world title four times 1981–84 and were the 1984 Olympic champions. They turned professional shortly thereafter, but returned to international competition in 1994 and immediately won the European Championship. They retired again from competitive ice dance after a bronze medal in the same year at the **Winter Olympics** in Lillehammer, Norway.

Totalizator or Tote

A system of betting on racehorses or greyhounds. All money received is divided in equal shares among winning ticket owners, less expenses.

Tottenham Hotspur FC
Hotspur FC was formed in 1882 by a group of cricketers (many were former pupils of Tottenham Grammar School), changing the name of the club two years later to Tottenham Hotspur. By 1899, 'Spurs' were playing at White Hart Lane, their home ground still today. The club has won the **FA Cup** eight times, the League Winners Cup twice, the European Cup Winners' Cup once, the **UEFA Cup** twice, and the Worthington Cup once. Famous players throughout the club's history include Sir **Alf Ramsey**, Ronnie Burgess, Danny Blanchflower, Jimmy Greaves, Pat Jennings, Terry Venables, Joe Kinnear, Glenn Hoddle, Ossie Ardiles, Chris Waddle, **Gary Lineker**, and **Paul Gascoigne**.

Tour de France
French road race for professional cyclists held annually over approximately 4,800 km/3,000 mi of primarily French roads. The race takes about three weeks to complete and the route varies each year, often taking in adjoining countries, but always ending in Paris. A separate stage is held every day, and the overall leader at the end of each stage wears the coveted **yellow jersey** (French *maillot jaune*). First held 1903, it is now the most watched sporting event in the world, with more than 10 million spectators.

trampolining
Gymnastics performed on a sprung canvas sheet that allows the performer to reach great heights before landing again. Marks are gained for carrying out difficult manoeuvres. Synchronized trampolining and tumbling are also popular forms of the sport.

Used as a circus or show-business act in the early part of the 20th century, trampolining developed as a sport from 1936 when George Nissen of the USA invented a prototype trampoline. Trampolining made its Olympic debut at the Sydney 2000 **Olympic Games**, with individual events for men and women.

Trent Bridge
Test cricket ground in Nottingham, home of the Nottinghamshire county side. One of the oldest cricket grounds in Britain, it was

opened in 1838. The ground covers approximately 2.5 hectares/6.2 acres and the present-day capacity is around 30,000. It has staged Test cricket since 1899. A crowd of 101,886 watched the England–Australia Test match in 1948.

triathlon

Test of stamina involving three sports: swimming, cycling, and running, each one immediately following the last. It was first established as a sport in the USA in 1974. There are various distances: sprint, olympic, half iron man, and iron man. The most celebrated event is the Hawaii Ironman for which competitors must swim 3.8 km/2.4 mi, cycle 180 km/112 mi, and run a full marathon - 42.195 km/26 mi 385 yd. Triathlon was an Olympic sport for the first time at the Sydney **Olympic Games** in 2000. The Olympic distance requires a 1,500 m/0.93 mi swim, a 40 km/24.85 mi cycle, and a 10 km/6.1 mi run.

triple jump

Track and field event in athletics comprising a hop, step, and jump sequence from a takeoff board into a sandpit landing area measuring 8 m/ 26.25 ft (minimum) in length. The takeoff board is usually 13 m/42.65 ft from the landing area. Each competitor has six trials and the winner is the one who covers the longest distance. (*See illustration on p. 165.*)

tug-of-war

The first recorded tug-of-war contest was around 2000 BC on an ancient wall engraving in Egypt. Western Europe took up the contest in AD 1000 with Scandinavia and Germany being the main contenders. The name tug-of-war is derived from the German words '*toga werra*' meaning 'a contest in tugging'. Until 1920, the tug-of-war was an Olympic contest, the gold medal often going to teams from Sweden, the USA, and Great Britain. Due to the **International Olympic Committee**'s decision to reduce the number of participants in the 1920 games, tug-of-war was deleted from the programme. However, tug-of-war has remained an international sport with the first World Championships in 1975. The sport was a founding disci-

triple jump *Jonathan Edwards of Great Britain executes the stages of the triple jump in the Barcelona Olympics, winning a silver medal.*

pline of the World Games of 1981, where Great Britain, Switzerland, and Ireland have since won gold medals.

Twickenham

Stadium in southwest London, the ground at which England play home **rugby union** internationals. It first staged an international match in 1910. The Rugby Football Union has its headquarters at Twickenham, and the **Harlequins** club used to play some of its home matches there. The ground was extensively rebuilt in the 1990s and now has a capacity of 75,000.

Tyson, Mike (Michael Gerald) (1966–   )

US heavyweight boxer, undisputed world champion from August 1987 to February 1990. He won the World Boxing Council heavyweight title 1986 when he beat Trevor Berbick to become the youngest world heavyweight champion. He beat James 'Bonecrusher' Smith for the World Boxing Association title in 1987 and later that year became the first undisputed champion since 1978 when he beat Tony Tucker for the International Boxing Federation title. Tyson had his boxing license revoked and was fined $3 mil-

CAREER HIGHLIGHTS

professional record fights
54; wins: 48 (42 inside the distance; defeats: 3; no result: 1.

lion in July 1997 for biting part of the ear off Evander Holyfield during the heavyweight championship fight on 28 June. He was disqualified during that event. In October 1998 he was given back his boxing license by the Nevada State Athletic Commission. In February 1999 he was jailed for 12 months following his violence towards two motorists during a car accident in Gaithesburgh, Maryland, in 1998. Tyson was convicted of rape and imprisoned 1992–95. He regained the World Boxing Council title 1996 when he defeated Frank **Bruno** in Las Vegas.

UEFA Cup

The UEFA Cup was first staged in 1958 as the Intercity Fairs Cup, changing its name to the UEFA Cup in 1972. Teams from Spain (eight), England (nine), and Italy (10) have dominated the competition, with **Real Madrid**, **Inter Milan**, Juventus, and **Barcelona** all winning three times.

ultimate frisbee

A fast-paced team sport played with a disc (or frisbee). The object of the sport is to score points by passing the disc from player to player until a pass is caught in the end zone for a goal. No running with the disc is allowed. Any incomplete passes or interceptions result in a turnover and the other team then gets a chance to score. Ultimate frisbee is a non-contact sport that requires a combination of agility, speed, and quickness to play. There are seven players from each team on the field at any one time.

ultra running

Ultra running is very long distance running; ultra marathons are any races longer than 26.2 mi/42.2 km, and ultra runs are long, difficult runs regardless of distance. Some ultra races are as far as 100 miles.

US PGA National Championships (golf)

The Professional Golfers Association of America was set up in 1916 by businessman Rodman Wanamaker, and operates a number of tournaments, including the PGA National Championship.

volleyball

Indoor and outdoor team game played on a court between two teams of six players each. A net is placed across the centre of the court, and players hit the ball with their hands over it, the aim being to ground it in the opponents' court. Originally called Mintonette, the game was invented in 1895 by William G Morgan in Massachusetts, USA, as a rival to the newly developed basketball. The playing area measures 18 m/59 ft by 9 m/29 ft 5 in. The ball, slightly smaller than a basketball, may not be hit more than three times on one team's side of the net without being hit to the other side. The sport's world governing body, the Fédération Internationale de Volley Ball (FIVB) was established in Paris in 1947. World championships, organized by FIVB, were first held in 1949 for men and 1952 for women, and are held every four years. Volleyball became an Olympic event in 1964.

volleyball, beach

Beach volleyball, a two-aside version of the game played on a sand court, emerged in California in the early 1930s. The first FIVB-sanctioned beach volleyball world championships took place in Brazil in 1986, and ten years later it became an Olympic event.

volleyball, beach *Nancy Reno (left) of the US spikes the ball as Brigitte Lesage of France attempts to block the shot at the 1996 Olympics. This was the first year beach volleyball was an Olympic medal sport.*

Wade, (Sarah) Virginia (1945–   )

English tennis player who won the **Wimbledon** singles title in the Silver Jubilee year of 1977. She also won the **US Open** in 1968 and the 1972 **Australian Open**. She holds a record number of appearances for the **Wightman** and **Federation Cup** teams and her total of eight **Grand Slam** titles is a post-war British record equalled only by Ann Jones.

wakeboarding

Recreational and competitive water sport in which a person is pulled across the surface of the water on a wakeboard, a symmetrically-shaped board usually about 1.2 m/4 ft long and 0.6 m/2 ft across the middle, by means of a tow rope attached to a speedboat. The wakeboarder, whose feet are strapped to the board with bindings, zigzags across the 'wake' (the ramp of water created by the pulling boat), and uses props such as take-off platforms to execute jumps, flips, and other manoeuvres. Some of these manoeuvres are similar to those performed in barefoot and freestyle **water skiing**, but others are derived from **surfing**, **snowboarding**, and **skateboarding**. In the 1990s wakeboarding was one of the world's fastest growing water sports.

walking, race

Race walking is a contest to cover a set distance faster than the opposition, while ensuring that at all times a part of the walker's foot is in contact with the ground so that no visible (to the human eye) loss of contact occurs. In addition, the advancing leg must be straight as soon as it makes contact with the ground – these two rules combine to create the slightly stiff-legged style, with little sideways movement. Failing to master these two requirements can lead to disqualification. Race walking has been an Olympic event since the early 1900s.

Wallabies, the

The nickname of the Australian **rugby union** test side, the Wallabies played their first test match in 1889 against a touring British side, though their great rivalry is with New Zealand (against whom they contest the Bledisloe Cup) and latterly South Africa, the three countries playing the southern hemisphere Tri-Nations tournament. Australia won the 1991 and 1999 **Rugby World Cups**, beating England 12–6 at Twickenham and France 35–12 at Cardiff. Great Wallabies include John Eales, **David Campese**, and the Ella brothers.

Walsh, Courtney Andrew (1962–)

West Indian **cricket** player. He made his Test debut in 1984 and by the end of March 1998 had taken 375 Test wickets. He captained the West Indies from 1996 to 1997. In 1997 he became only the sixth bowler to take 200 wickets in limited overs internationals. On 28 March 2000 playing on his home ground of Sabina Park, Jamaica, against Zimbabwe, he surpassed Kapil Dev's career total of 434 Test wickets to become the highest wicket taker in Test history.

Warne, Shane Keith (1969–)

Australian **cricket** player. In 1995 he took his 200th test wicket in only his 42nd test. By 2000 he had become ninth in Australia's all-time list of Test wicket takers, having overtaken Dennis Lillee's career total of 355 wickets in the Test against New Zealand on 15 March 2000. He helped Australia win the 1999 World Cup, winning the man of the match award in the final after returning figures of 4–33. He was also the tournament's joint top wicket taker with 20 wickets. In 1999 he became Australia's leading wicket taker in One-Day Internationals, overtaking Craig McDermott's total of 203 wickets. In April 2000 he was voted the fourth greatest cricketer of the 20th century by the Wisden Cricketers' Almanack, the only current player included in the top five.

Washington Redskins
American football team. Over the last 30 years they have won three **Super Bowls**, and 13 playoffs since 1971. First formed in 1932, the team was originally called the Boston Braves, then the Boston Redskins, and then in 1937 the team moved to Washington. The team took off when Joe Gibbs took over in 1981; the most successful coach in Washington history with a record of 140–65–0, eight playoff appearances, five NFC Eastern division championships, and three Super Bowl wins. Now playing out of Jack Kent Cooke Stadium, great Redskins include quarterbacks Sammy Baugh and Joe Theismann and running back John Riggins.

Waterloo Cup
The principal coursing event (chasing of hares by greyhounds) in England, known as the 'courser's Derby'. Staged at Altcar, near Formby, Merseyside, each year, it is named after the nearby Waterloo Hotel whose proprietor originated the race in 1936.

water polo
Water sport developed in England in 1869, originally called 'soccer-in-water'. The aim is to score goals, as in soccer, at each end of a swimming pool. It is played by teams of seven on each side (from squads of 13). An inflated ball is passed among the players, who must swim around the pool without touching the bottom. A goal is scored when the ball is thrown past the goalkeeper and into a net. The Swimming Association of Great Britain recognized the game in 1885. World championships were first held in 1973; they are held during the world swimming championships.

water skiing
Water sport in which a person is towed across water on a ski or skis (wider than those used for skiing on snow), or barefoot, by means of a rope attached to a speedboat. Competitions are held for overall performances, slalom, tricks, jumping, and racing.

In 1922 Ralph Samuelson (US) pioneered the sport as it is known today. Water skiing's international governing body is the

International Water Ski Federation (IWSF). This replaced the World Water Ski Union (WWSU), formed in 1946 as the Union Internationale de Ski Nautique. World championships were first held in 1949 and are now staged every two years.

weightlifting

Sport of lifting the heaviest possible weight above one's head to the satisfaction of judges. In international competitions there are two standard lifts: snatch and jerk.

In the snatch, the bar and weights are lifted from the floor to a position with the arms outstretched and above the head in one continuous movement. The arms must be locked for two seconds for the lift to be good. The jerk is a two-movement lift: from the floor to the chest, and from the chest to the outstretched position. The aggregate weight of the two lifts counts. The International Weightlifting Federation was formed in 1920, although a world championship was first held in 1891. The first women's world championship was held in 1987 in Florida, USA.

Weissmuller, Johnny (Peter John) (1904–1984)

US swimmer and film actor. He won three Olympic gold medals in 1924 and two more in 1928. He set freestyle world records at every distance between 100 yards and half a mile, many of them by remarkable margins. The first person to swim the 100 metres in under a minute and the 400 metres in less than five minutes, he transformed freestyle swimming in the 1920s with his revolutionary high crawl style. As an actor he played Edgar Rice Burroughs's rainforest hero Tarzan in a long-running series of films for Metro-Goldwyn-Mayer and RKO in the 1930s and 1940s. He later starred in the *Jungle Jim* series of B films.

Wembley Stadium

Sports ground in north London, England, completed in 1923 for the British Empire Exhibition 1924–25. It has been the scene of the annual **FA Cup** final since 1923. The 1948 **Olympic Games** and many concerts, including the Live Aid concert of 1985, were held here. Adjacent to the main stadium, which holds 79,000 people all seated, is the Wembley indoor arena (which holds about 10,000, depending on the event). Wembley is to be completely rebuilt at an estimated cost of £475 million. The new 90,000 capacity stadium, designed by a group of architects headed by Norman Foster, is scheduled to be ready in March 2003. The largest recorded crowd at Wembley is 126,047 for its first FA Cup final; the capacity has since been reduced by additional seating. England play most of their home soccer matches at Wembley. Other sports events held at Wembley Stadium over the years have included show jumping, **American football**, **rugby league**, **rugby union**, **hockey**, **Gaelic football**, **hurling**, and **baseball**.

wheelchair basketball
First played by disabled US veterans of World War II, the sport is now international with the event contested at the **Paralympic Games** by national sides, and with the creation of a Gold Cup for the world's top men's teams.

wheelchair rugby or quad rugby
Developed in Canada, wheelchair rugby was first called murderball and the first national championship was played in 1979. Currently the fastest-growing wheelchair sport, the game operates by classifying players according to their disability level, with seven classes ranging from 0.5–3.5. Each team can have four players on a modified basketball court at any one time, whose combined disability level is 8.0 or less. This allows people of different disabilities and sexes to play together. The object is to take the ball into the opposition's half and cross the goal line, passing the ball between players. A player can only hold the ball for 10 seconds before having to pass or dribble the ball – or possession is awarded to the other side.

wheelchair tennis
Wheelchair tennis appeared for the first time on the **Paralympic Games** programme in 1992 after being developed in the USA. It follows traditional tennis rules with both singles and doubles events;

the only difference is that the players are allowed two bounces of the ball (with the first bounce being within the bounds of the court).

whist
Card game for four, predecessor of bridge, in which the partners try to win a majority of the 13 tricks (the highest card played being the winner of the trick).

Whitbread, Fatima (1961–)
Adoptive name of Fatima Vedad, English javelin thrower. Powerfully built, though comparatively short in stature, Whitbread won an Olympic bronze in 1984 and in 1985 became the first woman to throw a javelin over 76 m/ 249 ft. She set a world record of over 77 m/253 ft the following year (the record was broken by Petra Felke at nearly 80 m/262 ft). She took the world championship title in Rome in 1987 and the Olympic silver medal in 1988.

Widnes RLFC
Once nicknamed 'the Chemics' (reflecting their position in England's industrial chemical heartland), Widnes Vikings enjoyed a flurry of success in the 1980s, and remain one of **rugby league's** major teams. Honours include three John Player Trophy titles, seven Lancashire Cups, three Division One Championships, and the World Club Challenge Trophy.

Wigan RLFC
Wigan Rugby Union Club was founded in 1872, and by 1879 had become Wigan Wasps. When the Northern Union was formed in 1895 by clubs that supported the principle of 'broken time payments', Wigan joined the **rugby league** code. Now known as the Warriors, club honours include winning the World Club Challenge (three times), the Superleague, the rugby league Championship (eight times), the first division Championship (seven times), and the Challenge Cup (15 times). Great players include Billy Boston, Ellery **Hanley**, Joe Lydon, and Shaun Edwards.

Wightman Cup
Annual **tennis** competition between international women's teams from the USA and the UK. The trophy, first contested in 1923, was donated by Hazel Hotchkiss Wightman (1886–1974), a former US tennis player who won singles, doubles, and mixed-doubles titles in the US Championships 1909–11. Because of US domination of the contest it was abandoned in 1990.

Williams, J(ohn) P(eter) R(hys) (1949–)
Welsh rugby union player. He won 55 caps for Wales and a further eight for the **British Lions**. He played in three Grand Slam winning teams and twice toured with winning British Lions teams. He played for St Mary's Hospital, Bridgend, and London Welsh. He also made history when he became the first international player to play both as a back and a forward, moving forward to play as a replacement flanker when Wales were on tour.

Wimbledon
English lawn **tennis** centre used for international championship matches, situated in south London. There are currently 18 courts. The first centre was at Worple Road when it was the home of the All England Croquet Club. Tennis was first played there in 1875, and in 1877 the club was renamed the All England Lawn Tennis and Croquet Club. The first all England championship was held in the same year. The club and championship moved to their present site in Church Road in 1922.

Windsurfing or boardsailing or sailboarding
Water sport combining elements of **surfing** and sailing, first developed in the USA in 1968. The windsurfer stands on a board that is propelled and steered by means of a sail attached to a mast that is articulated at the foot. Since 1984 the sport has been included in the **Olympic Games** as part of the yachting events. From 1992 men and women have competed in separate categories. There are also annual windsurfing world championships.

Winter Olympics

A four-yearly series of sports competitions on snow and ice, first held in 1924, and organized like the summer Olympics under the auspices of the **International Olympic Committee**. Although figure skating became an Olympic sport at the 1908 London Games and ice hockey was added in 1920, the first separate, self-contained Winter Olympic Games were held at Chamonix, France, in 1924, when 258 competitors from 16 nations competed for medals in Nordic skiing, ski jumping, **ice hockey**, four-man **bobsledding**, and figure and **speed skating**. Alpine skiing, which today attracts the most attention, was not introduced until 1936. Among the other sports to be introduced as medal events at subsequent games were the biathlon (1960), ice dancing (1976), and freestyle skiing (1992). The 1998 **Winter Olympics** in Nagano, Japan, were estimated to be the largest to date, with over 2,400 athletes from a record 72 countries taking part.

Witt, Katarina (1965–)

German ice-skater. She was 1984 Olympic champion (representing East Germany) and by 1990 had won four world titles (1984–85, 1987–88) and six consecutive European titles (1983–88). After four years as a professional she returned to competitive skating in 1993.

Woods, Tiger (1976–)

Born Eldrick Woods, US golfer. He has made a phenomenal impact on the game since 1994 when he became the youngest player, at the age of 18, to win the US Amateur Championship, the first of an unprecedented

Woods *Tiger Woods, US golfing star.*

three successive titles. Previously he had won the US Junior Championship on three successive occasions 1991–93. After his third Amateur Champion-ship triumph, he turned professional in 1996, immediately becoming one of the wealthiest men in US sport as a result of endorsement deals worth £40 million/$64 million.

In his first six months as a professional he won four tournaments on the US PGA circuit, then in 1997 he won the Mercedes Championships, the Honda Asian Classic (Bangkok), and the US Masters. Woods was voted the 1997 Associated Press Male Athlete of the Year, only the 5th golfer to win this award and the first since Lee Trevino. In February 2000, he became the first player to win six successive tournaments on the US PGA Tour since Ben Hogan in 1948.

> **CAREER HIGHLIGHTS**
>
> *US Amateur*
> 1994–96
>
> *US Masters*
> 1997
>
> *US PGA championship*
> 1999
>
> *US Open*
> 2000
>
> *British Open*
> 2000
>
> *Tournament wins*
> 21

World Cup (athletics)

A 'different' sort of world championships, as it is not the premier athletics event – the Olympic games fills that role. The World Cup is a regional event, with 'area' teams from Africa, the Americas, Europe, Oceania, and the USA – together with the top two men's and women's teams from the European and Europa Cups in a three-day match. Each team enters only one competitor per event. Initially held every two years, in 1985 the format was switched to a four-year cycle.

World Cup (football)

The world's top international football competition held every four years. It was first staged in 1930 when it was won by Uruguay, and last staged in France in 1998 when it was won by the hosts. The teams first played for the Jules Rimet trophy, but after Brazil won for the third time in 1970 they kept the cup and a new trophy, the FIFA World Cup was unveiled. Brazil has won the Cup four times, Italy and Germany three times, and Argentina and Uruguay twice. The only other country to win the World Cup was England in 1966, when the UK staged the competition. The 2002 Cup will be staged in Korea and Japan, and though the 2006 games have been awarded to Germany, the bid process is likely to be challenged legally.

World Series
Annual **baseball** competition between the winning teams of the National League (NL) and American League (AL). It is a best-of-seven series played each October. The first World Series was played in 1903 (as a best-of-nine series): the AL's Boston Pilgrims defeated the NL's Pittsburgh Pirates in eight games.

World Student Games (athletics)
Now held every two years, the first International Universities Games was held in Paris in 1923, though it was not until 1957 that the first 'official' Universiade was held, again in Paris. Britain hosted the games at Sheffield in 1991, and the 2001 games are due to be held in Beijing.

World Wrestling Federation (WWF)
A professional **wrestling** body staging fights, many of which are broadcast on satellite television. Fighters include 'Stone Cold' Steve Austin and Jeff Hardy.

wrestling
Sport popular in ancient Egypt, Greece, and Rome, and included in the Olympics from 704 BC. The two main modern international styles are Greco-Roman, concentrating on above-waist holds, and freestyle, which allows the legs to be used to hold or trip; in both the aim is to throw the opponent to the ground. Many countries have their own forms of wrestling. *Glima* is unique to Iceland; *Kushti* is the national style practised in Iran; *Schwingen* has been

practised in Switzerland for hundreds of years; and *sumo* is the national sport of Japan.

Wright, Billy (William Ambrose) (1924–1994)

English footballer. He won 105 caps for England 1946–59 including a record 90 as captain. He made 490 appearances for Wolverhampton Wanderers 1946–59, and led the club to the **FA Cup** in 1949 and the league championship in 1954, 1958, and 1959.

yachting

Pleasure cruising or racing a small and light vessel, whether sailed and powered by the wind or power-driven. At the 1996 **Olympic Games** there were eight sail-driven categories: Laser, 470, Tornado, Soling, Mistral, Star, Finn, and Europe. The Laser, Mistral, Finn, and Europe are solo events; the Soling class is for three-person crews; all other classes are for crews of two. The International Sailing Federation (ISF) World Sailing Championships were inaugurated in 1994 and are held every four years. Additionally, separate world championships are held annually in each of the Olympic classes and in others such as the Melges 24 or Mumm 30.

yachting, sand

Sand yachts are small sailing dinghies, mounted on a simple chassis with three or four car wheels. The boats are then propelled by the wind over sand, tarmac, concrete, or other level surfaces. The sail is operated as it would be on water, and the vehicle is steered by a steering wheel or pedals.

Yankee Stadium

Nicknamed 'The House That Ruth Built', the 57,545-seat stadium sits on a bend in the Harlem River. On its opening day, Babe **Ruth** hit a home run at Yankee Stadium, and since then it has been the venue for Don Larson's perfect game in the **World Series**, David Wells' perfect game in May of '98, and Reggie Jackson's playoff heroics. However, the Yankees may be moving to a new home, either in Manhattan or New Jersey. **See also:** *New York Yankees.*

yellow jersey

A yellow racing singlet worn by the overall leader of the **Tour de**

France, first awarded during the 1919 race. The jersey was yellow to match the paper used to print L'Auto (Automobile Cyclisme), a French newspaper about bike racing.

Zatopek, Emil (1922–2000)
Czech runner. At the **Olympic Games** in Helsinki 1952 he won gold medals for the 5,000 metres, the 10,000 metres, and the marathon. He retired as a runner in 1958, having set 18 world records during his career, including those for 10 miles, 15 miles, and 30,000 metres. He broke 13 world long-distance records between 1948 and 1954, winning the gold medal for the 10,000 metres world record of 28:54.2 in 1949.

Zelezny, Jan (1966–)
Czech Republic athlete. Twice world champion in the javelin event, Zelezny is credited with the best five throws in history, the best being his 98 m/323 ft throw in May 1996 that is the current world record. He won gold medals at the 1992 and 1996 Olympic Games. He increased his Olympic gold medal tally by winning the javelin event at the Sydney Olympic Games 2000. Once more he denied Britain's Steve Backley an Olympic crown; Backley broke the Olympic record only for the Czech to throw even further in one of the best-ever Olympic throws finals.

Appendix

Men's Outdoor Athletics World Records

As of 10 June 2000.

Category	Record	Name(s)	Country	Date	Location
Track					
100 m	9.79	Maurice Greene	USA	16 June 1999	Athens, Greece
200 m	19.32	Michael Johnson	USA	1 August 1996	Atlanta (GA), USA
400 m	43.18	Michael Johnson	USA	26 August 1999	Seville, Spain
800 m	1:41.11	Wilson Kipketer	Denmark	24 August 1997	Cologne, Germany
1,000 m	2:11.96	Noah Ngeny	Kenya	5 September 1999	Rieti, Italy
1,500 m	3:26.00	Hicham El Guerrouj	Morocco	17 July 1998	Rome, Italy
Mile	3:43.13	Hicham El Guerrouj	Morocco	7 July 1999	Rome, Italy
2,000 m	4:44.79	Hicham El Guerrouj	Morocco	7 September 1999	Berlin, Germany
3,000 m	7:20.67	Daniel Komen	Kenya	1 September 1996	Rieti, Italy
5,000 m	12:39.36	Haile Gebrselassie	Ethiopia	13 June 1998	Helsinki, Finland
10,000 m	26:22.75	Haile Gebrselassie	Ethiopia	1 June 1998	Hengelo, Netherlands
20,000 m	56:55.60	Arturo Barrios	Mexico	30 March 1991	La Flèche, France
25,000 m	1 h 13:55.80	Toshihiko Seko	Japan	22 March 1981	Christchurch, New Zealand
3,000 m steeplechase	7:55.72	Bernard Barmasai	Kenya	24 August 1997	Cologne, Germany

Category	Record	Name(s)	Country	Date	Location
Half marathon	59:17	Paul Tergat	Kenya	4 April 1998	Milan, Italy
Marathon	2 h 5:42	Khalid Khannouchi	Morocco	24 October 1999	Chicago, USA
110-m hurdles	12.91	Colin Jackson	Great Britain	20 August 1993	Stuttgart, Germany
400-m hurdles	46.78	Kevin Young	USA	6 August 1992	Barcelona, Spain
4 x 100-m relay	37.40	Marsh, Burrell, Mitchell, Lewis	USA	8 August 1992	Barcelona, Spain
		Drummond, Cason, Mitchell, Burrell	USA	21 August 1993	Stuttgart, Germany
4 x 200-m relay	1:18.68	Marsh, Burrell, Heard, Lewis	USA	17 April 1994	Walnut (CA), USA
4 x 400-m relay	2:54.29	Valmon, Watts, Reynolds, Johnson	USA	22 August 1993	Stuttgart, Germany
4 x 800-m relay	7:03.89	Elliott, Cook, Cram, Coe	Great Britain	30 August 1982	London, UK

Field

Category	Record	Name(s)	Country	Date	Location
High jump	2.45 m/ 8 ft 1/2 in	Javier Sotomayor	Cuba	27 July 1993	Salamanca, Spain
Long jump	8.95 m/ 29 ft 41/2 in	Mike Powell	USA	30 August 1991	Tokyo, Japan
Triple jump	18.29 m/ 60 ft 1/4 in	Jonathan Edwards	Great Britain	7 August 1995	Gothenburg, Sweden
Pole vault	6.14 m/ 20 ft 13/4 in	Sergei Bubka	Ukraine	31 July 1994	Sestriere, Italy
Shot put	23.12 m/ 75 ft 10 1/4 in	Randy Barnes	USA	20 May 1990	Los Angeles (CA), USA
Discus	74.08 m/ 243 ft	Jürgen Schult	East Germany	6 June 1986	Neubrandenburg, Germany

Category	Record	Name(s)	Country	Date	Location
Javelin	98.48 m/ 323 ft 1 in	J·n Zelezny	Czech Republic	25 May 1996	Jena, Germany
Hammer	86.74 m/ 284 ft 7 in	Yuri Sedykh	USSR	30 August 1986	Stuttgart, Germany
Decathlon	8,894 pts1	Thomas Dvorak	Czech	4 July 1999	Prague, Czech Republic
20-km walk	1 h 17:25.6	Bernardo Segura	Mexico	7 May 1994	Bergen, Norway
30-km walk	2 h 01:44.1	Maurizio Damilano	Italy	3 October 1992	Cuneo, Italy
50-km walk	3 h 40:57.9	Thierry Toutain	France	29 September 1996	Héricourt, France

Women's Outdoor Athletics World Records

As of 10 June 2000.

Category	Record	Name	Country	Date	Location
Track					
100 m	10.49	Florence Griffith-Joyner	USA	16 July 1988	Indianapolis (IN), USA
200 m	21.34	Florence Griffith-Joyner	USA	29 September 1988	Seoul, South Korea
400 m	47.60	Marita Koch	East Germany	6 October 1985	Canberra, Australia
800 m	1:53.28	Jarmila Kratochvìlov·	Czechos-lovakia	26 July 1983	Munich, West Germany
1,000 m	2:28.98	Svetlana Masterkova	Russia	23 August 1996	Brussels, Belgium
1,500 m	3:50.46	Cu Yunxia	China	11 September 1993	Beijing, China
Mile	4:12.56	Svetlana Masterkova	Russia	14 August 1996	Zurich, Switzerland
2,000 m	5:25.36	Sonia O'Sullivan	Ireland, Republic of	9 July 1994	Edinburgh, UK
3,000 m	8:06.11	Wang Junxia	China	13 September 1993	Beijing, China
5,000 m	14:28.09	Jiang Bo	China	23 October 1997	Shanghai, China
10,000 m	29:31.78	Wang Junxia	China	8 September 1993	Beijing, China
Half marathon	1 h 06:43	Masako Chika	Japan	19 April 1997	Tokyo, Japan
Marathon	2 h 20:43.00	Tegla Loroupe	Kenya	26 September 1999	Berlin, Germany
100-m hurdles	12.21	Yordanka Donkova	Bulgaria	21 August 1988	Stara Zagora, Bulgaria
400-m hurdles	52.61	Kim Batten	USA	11 August 1995	Gothenburg, Sweden

Category	Record	Name	Country	Date	Location
4 x 100-m relay	41.37	Gladisch, Rieger, Auerswald, Göhr	East Germany	6 October 1985	Canberra, Australia
4 x 200-m relay	1:27.461	Jenkins, Collander, Perry, Jones	USA "Blue"Team	29 April 2000	Philadelphia (PA), USA
4 x 400-m relay	3:15.17	Ledovskaya, Nazarova, Pinigina, Bryzgina	USSR	1 October 1988	Seoul, South Korea
4 x 800-m relay	7:50.17	Olizarenko, Gurina, Borisova, Podyalovskaya	USSR	5 August 1984	Moscow, Russian Federation
Field					
High jump	2.09 m/ 6 ft 10 1/4 in	Stefka Kostadinova	Bulgaria	30 August 1987	Rome, Italy
Long jump	7.52 m/ 24 ft 8 1/4 in	Galina Chistyakova	USSR	11 June 1988	Leningrad, Russian Federation
Triple jump	15.50 m/ 50 ft 101/4 in	Inessa Kravets	Ukraine	10 August 1995	Gothenburg, Sweden
Pole vault	4.62 m/ 15 ft 2 in[1]	Stacy Dragila	USA	27 May 2000	Phoenix (AZ), USA
Shot put	22.64 m/ 74 ft 3 in	Natalya Lisovskaya	USSR	7 June 1987	Moscow, Russian Federation
Discus	76.80 m/ 252 ft	Gabriele Reinsch	East Germany	9 July 1988	Neubrandenburg, Germany
Hammer	76.07 m/ 249 ft 6 in	Michaela Melinte	Romania	29 August 1999	Rülingen, Switzerland
Javelin	67.09 m/ 220 ft 11/2 in	Mirela Manjani-Tzelili	Greece	28 August 1999	Seville, Spain
Heptathlon	7,291 pts	Jackie Joyner-Kersee	USA	23–24 September 1988	Seoul, South Korea
5-km walk	20:13.26	Kerry Saxby-Junna	Australia	25 February 1996	Hobart, Australia
10-km walk	41:56.23	Nadezhda Ryashkina	USSR	24 July 1990	Seattle (WA), USA

[1] Awaiting ratification.

Men's Athletics: Olympic Gold Medalists 2000

Event	Winner	Country	Time/score/distance
100 m	Maurice Green	USA	9.87
200 m	Konstantinos Kenteris	Greece	20.09
400 m	Michael Johnson	USA	43:84
800 m	Nils Schumann	Germany	1:45.08
1,500 m	Noah Ngeny	Kenya	3:32.07
5,000 m	Millon Wolde	Ethiopia	13:35.49
10,000 m	Haile Gebrselassie	Ethiopia	27:18.20
Marathon	Gezahgne Abera	Ethiopia	2 h 10:11.00
110-m hurdles	Anier Garcia	Cuba	13.00
400-m hurdles	Angelo Taylor	USA	47.50
20 km walk	Robert Korzeniowski	Poland	1 h 18:59.00
50 km walk	Robert Korzeniowski	Poland	3 h 42:22.00
300-m steeplechase	Rueben Kosgei	Kenya	8:21.43
High jump	Sergey Kliugin	Russia	2.35 m/7 ft 8$\frac{1}{2}$ in
Pole vault	Nick Hysong	USA	5.90 m/19 ft 4$\frac{1}{4}$ in
Long jump	Ivan Pedroso	Cuba	8.55 m/28 ft $\frac{1}{2}$ in
Triple jump	Jonathan Edwards	Great Britain	17.71 m/58ft 1 in
Shot put	Arsi Harju	Finland	21.29m/69 ft 9 in
Discus	Virgilijus Alekna	Lithuania	69.30 m/227 ft 4 in
Hammer	Szymon Ziolowski	Poland	80.02 m/262 ft 6 in
Javelin	Jan Zeleny	Czech Republic	90.17 m/295 ft 10 in
Decathlon	Erki Nool	Estonia	8,641 points
4 x 100-m relay		USA	37.61
4 x 400-m relay		USA	2:56:35

Women's Athletics: Olympic Gold Medalists 2000

Event	Winner	Country	Time/score/distance
100 m	Marion Jones	USA	10.75
200 m	Marion Jones	USA	21.84
400 m	Cathy Freeman	Australia	49.11
800 m	Maria Mutola	Mozambique	1:56.15
1,500 m	Nouria Merah-Benida	Algeria	4:05.10
5,000 m	Gabrielaa Szabo	Romania	14:40.10
10,000 m	Derartu Tulu	Ethiopia	30:17.49
Marathon	Naoko Takahashi	Japan	2 h 23:14
110-m hurdles	Olga Shishingina	Kazakhstan	12.65
400-m hurdles	Irina Privalova	Russia	53.02
20-km walk	Wang Liping	China	1 hr 29.05
High jump	Yelena Yelesina	Russia	2.01 m/6 ft 7$^3/_4$ in
Pole vault	Stacey Dragila	USA	4.60 m/15 ft 1 in
Long jump	Heike Dreschler	Germany	6.99 m/22 ft 11 in
Triple jump	Tereza Marinova	Bulgaria	15.20 m/49 ft 10 in
Shot put	Yanina Korolchik	Belarus	20.56 m/67 ft 5$^1/_2$ in
Discus	Ellina Zvereva	Belarus	68.40 m/224 ft 4$^3/_4$ in
Hammer	Kamila Skolimowska	Poland	71.16 m/233 ft 5 in
Javelin	Trine Hattestad	Norway	68.91 m/226 ft 1 in
Pentathlon	Nadyezda Tkachenko	USSR	5,083 points
Heptathlon	Denise Lewis	Great Britain	6.584 points
4 x 100-m relay		Bahamas	41.95
4 x 400-m relay		USA	3:22.62

Summer Olympics 2000 Final Medal Table

Position	Country	Gold	Silver	Bronze	Total
1	USA	39	25	33	97
2	Russia	32	28	28	88
3	China	28	16	15	59
4	Austria	16	25	17	58
5	Germany	14	17	26	57
6	France	13	14	11	38
7	Italy	13	8	13	34
8	Netherlands	12	9	4	25
9	Cuba	11	11	7	29
10	Great Britain	11	10	7	28
11	Romania	11	6	9	26
12	South Korea	8	9	11	28
13	Hungary	8	6	3	17
14	Poland	6	5	3	14
15	Japan	5	8	5	18
16	Bulgaria	5	6	2	13
17	Greece	4	6	3	13
18	Sweden	4	5	3	12
19	Norway	4	3	3	10
20	Ethiopia	4	1	3	8
21	Ukraine	3	10	10	23
22	Kazakhstan	3	4	0	7
23	Belarus	3	3	11	17
24	Canada	3	3	8	14
25	Spain	3	3	5	11
26=	Iran	3	0	1	4
	Turkey	3	0	1	4
28	Czech Republic	2	3	3	8
29	Kenya	2	3	2	7
30	Denmark	2	3	1	6
31	Finland	2	1	1	4
32	Austria	2	1	0	3
33	Lithuania	2	0	3	5
34	Azerbaijan	2	0	1	3
35	Slovenia	2	0	0	2

Position	Country	Gold	Silver	Bronze	Total
36	Switzerland	1	6	2	9
37	Indonesia	1	3	2	6
38	Slovakia	1	3	1	5
39	Mexico	1	2	3	6
40	Algeria	1	1	3	5
41	Uzbekistan	1	1	2	4
42=	Latvia	1	1	1	3
	Yugoslavia	1	1	1	3
44	Bahamas	1	1	0	2
45	New Zealand	1	0	3	4
46=	Estonia	1	0	2	3
	Thailand	1	0	2	3
48	Croatia	1	0	1	2
49=	Cameroon	1	0	0	1
	Colombia	1	0	0	1
	Mozambique	1	0	0	1
52	Brazil	1	6	6	12
53	Jamaica	0	4	3	7
54	Nigeria	0	3	0	3
55=	Belgium	0	2	3	5
	South Africa	0	2	3	5
57	Argentina	0	2	2	4
58=	Morocco	0	1	4	5
	Chinese Taipei	0	1	4	5
60	North Korea	0	1	3	4
61=	Saudi Arabia	0	1	1	2
	Moldova	0	1	1	2
	Trnidad and Tobago	0	1	1	2
64=	Ireland, Republic of	0	1	0	1
	Uruguay	0	1	0	1
	Vietnam	0	1	0	1
67=	Georgia	0	0	6	6
	Costa Rica	0	0	2	2
	Portugal	0	0	2	2
70=	Armenia	0	0	1	1
	Barbados	0	0	1	1
	Chile	0	0	1	1
	India	0	0	1	1

Position	Country	Gold	Silver	Bronze	Total
	Iceland	0	0	1	1
	Israel	0	0	1	1
	Kyrgyzstan	0	0	1	1
	Kuwait	0	0	1	1
	Macedonia	0	0	1	1
	Qatar	0	0	1	1
	Sri Lanka	0	0	1	1
	Total	301	299	328	928

Men's Swimming: Olympic Gold Medalists 2000

Event	Name	Country	Time
50 m freestyle	Gary Hall	USA	21.98
	Anthony Erwin	USA	
100 m freestyle	Pieter van den Hoogenband	Netherlands	48.30
200 m freestyle	Pieter van den Hoogenband	Netherlands	1:45.35
400 m freestyle	Ian Thorpe	Australia	3:40.59
1,500 m freestyle	Grant Hacket	Australia	14:48.33
100 m breaststroke	Domenico Fioravanti	Italy	1:00.46
200 m breaststroke	Domenico Fioravanti	Italy	2:10.87
100 m backstroke	Lenny Krayzelburg	USA	53.72
200 m backstroke	Lenny Krayzelburg	USA	1:56.76
100 m butterfly	Lars Froelander	Sweden	52.00
200 m butterfly	Tom Malchow	USA	1:55.35
200 m individual medley	Massimiliano Rosolino	Italy	1:58.98
400 m individual medley	Tom Dolan	USA	4:11.76
4 x 100-m freestyle		Australia	3:13.67
4 x 200-m freestyle		Australia	7:07.05
4 x 100-m medley relay		USA	3:33.73

Women's Swimming: Olympic Gold Medalists 2000

Event	Name	Country	Time
50 m freestyle	Inge de Bruijn	Netherlands	24.32
100 m freestyle	Inge de Bruijn	Netherlands	53.82
200 m freestyle	Susie O'Neil	Australia	1:58.24
400 m freestyle	Brooke Bennett	USA	4:05.80
1,500 m freestyle	Brooke Bennett	USA	8:19.67
100 m breaststroke	Megan Quann	USA	1:07.05
200 m breaststroke	Agnes Kovacs	Hungary	2:24.35
100 m backstroke	Diana Mocanu	Romania	1:00.21
200 m backstroke	Diana Mocanu	Romania	2:08.16
100 m butterfly	Inge de Bruijn	Netherlands	56.61
200 m butterfly	Misty Hyman	USA	2:05.88
200 m individual medley	Yana Klochkova	Ukraine	2:10.68
400 m individual medley	Yana Klochkova	Ukraine	4:33.59
4 x 100-m freestyle		USA	3:36.61
4 x 200-m freestyle		USA	7:57.80
4 x 100-m medley relay		USA	3:58.30

World Series Records

(− = not applicable.)

Record	Player	Team	Score/average	Date
Most world series appearances by a team	−	New York Yankees	34	−
Most world series wins by a team	−	New York Yankees	23	−
Best career batting average	Lou Brock	St Louis Cardinals	.391	−
Best batting average during a series	Billy Hatcher	Cincinnati Reds	.750	1990
Most career home runs	Mickey Mantle	New York Yankees	18	1997
Most home runs in a series	Reggie Jackson	New York Yankees	5	−
Most home runs in a single game	Babe Ruth	New York Yankees	3	6 October 1926 and 9 October 1928
	Reggie Jackson	New York Yankees		18 October 1977
Most career hits	Yogi Berra	New York Yankees	71	−
Most hits in a series	Bobby Richardson	New York Yankees	13	1960
	Lou Brock	St Louis Cardinals		1968
	Marty Barrett	Boston Red Sox		1986
Most career runs batted in (RBIs)	Mickey Mantle	New York Yankees	40	−
Most RBIs in a series	Bobby Richardson	New York Yankees	12	1960
Most RBIs in a single game	Bobby Richardson	New York Yankees	6	1960
Perfect games pitched in World Series	Don Larsen	New York Yankees	1	1956

Record	Player	Team	Score/ average	Date
Most career wins by a pitcher	Whitey Ford	New York Yankees	10	–
Most career strikeouts	Whitey Ford	New York Yankees	94	–
Most strikeouts in a series	Bob Gibson	St Louis Cardinals	35	1968
Most strikeouts in a game	Bob Gibson	St Louis Cardinals	17	1968
Most innings pitched in a career	Whitey Ford	New York Yankees	146	–
Most innings pitched in a game	Babe Ruth	New York Yankees	14	1916
Most career saves	Rollie Fingers	Oakland Athletics	6	–
Most saves during a series	John Wetteland	New York Yankees	4	–

Yachting: Admiral's Cup Winners

Year	Country	Year	Country
1969	USA	1985	West Germany
1971	UK	1987	New Zealand
1973	West Germany	1989	UK
1975	UK	1991	France
1977	UK	1993	Germany
1979	Australia	1995	Italy
1981	UK	1997	USA
1983	West Germany	1999	Netherlands

Formula 1 World Drivers' Championship Winners

This championship was inaugurated in 1950.

Year	Name	Country	Car
1950	Giuseppe Farina	Italy	Alfa Romeo
1951	Juan Manuel Fangio	Argentina	Alfa Romeo
1952	Alberto Ascari	Italy	Ferrari
1953	Alberto Ascari	Italy	Ferrari
1954	Juan Manuel Fangio	Argentina	Maserati-Mercedes
1955	Juan Manuel Fangio	Argentina	Mercedes-Benz
1956	Juan Manuel Fangio	Argentina	Lancia-Ferrari
1957	Juan Manuel Fangio	Argentina	Maserati
1958	Mike Hawthorn	UK	Ferrari
1959	Jack Brabham	Australia	Cooper-Climax
1960	Jack Brabham	Australia	Cooper-Climax
1961	Phil Hill	USA	Ferrari
1962	Graham Hill	UK	BRM
1963	Jim Clark	UK	Lotus-Climax
1964	John Surtees	UK	Ferrari
1965	Jim Clark	UK	Lotus-Climax
1966	Jack Brabham	Australia	Brabham-Repco
1967	Denny Hulme	New Zealand	Brabham-Repco
1968	Graham Hill	UK	Lotus-Ford
1969	Jackie Stewart	UK	Matra-Ford
1970	Jochen Rindt	Austria	Lotus-Ford
1971	Jackie Stewart	UK	Tyrrell-Ford
1972	Emerson Fittipaldi	Brazil	Lotus-Ford
1973	Jackie Stewart	UK	Tyrrell-Ford

Year	Name	Country	Car
1974	Emerson Fittipaldi	Brazil	McLaren-Ford
1975	Niki Lauda	Austria	Ferrari
1976	James Hunt	UK	McLaren-Ford
1977	Niki Lauda	Austria	Ferrari
1978	Mario Andretti	USA	Lotus-Ford
1979	Jody Scheckter	South Africa	Ferrari
1980	Alan Jones	Australia	Williams-Ford
1981	Nelson Piquet	Brazil	Brabham-Ford
1982	Keke Rosberg	Finland	Williams-Ford
1983	Nelson Piquet	Brazil	Brabham-BMW
1984	Niki Lauda	Austria	McLaren-TAG
1985	Alain Prost	France	McLaren-TAG
1986	Alain Prost	France	McLaren-TAG
1987	Nelson Piquet	Brazil	Williams-Honda
1988	Ayrton Senna	Brazil	McLaren-Honda
1989	Alain Prost	France	McLaren-Honda
1990	Ayrton Senna	Brazil	McLaren-Honda
1991	Ayrton Senna	Brazil	McLaren-Honda
1992	Nigel Mansell	UK	Williams-Renault
1993	Alain Prost	France	Williams-Renault
1994	Michael Schumacher	Germany	Benetton-Ford
1995	Michael Schumacher	Germany	Benetton-Renault
1996	Damon Hill	UK	Williams-Renault
1997	Jacques Villeneuve	Canada	Williams-Renault
1998	Mika Hakkinen	Finland	McLaren-Mercedes
1999	Mika Hakkinen	Finland	McLaren-Mercedes
2000	Michael Schumacher	Germany	Ferrari

Men's US Open Golf Championship Winners

The US Open was first held on a 9-hole course at Newport (RI), USA, in 1895; the winner was English–born Horace Rawlins.

Year	Name	Country	Location	Score
1990	Hale Irwin	USA	Medinah (IL)	280[1]
1991	Payne Stewart	USA	Hazeltine (MN)	282[1]
1992	Tom Kite	USA	Monterey (CA)	285
1993	Lee Janzen	USA	Baltusrol (NJ)	272
1994	Ernie Els	South Africa	Oakmont (PA)	279
1995	Corey Pavin	USA	Shinnecock Hills (NY)	280
1996	Steve Jones	USA	Oakland Hills (MI)	278
1997	Ernie Els	South Africa	Congressional (MI)	276
1998	Lee Janzen	USA	Olympic Club (CA)	280
1999	Payne Stewart	USA	Pinehurst (NC)	279
2000	Tiger Woods	USA	Pebble Beach (CA)	272

[1] Score after play-off.

Tour de France Winners

This race was first held in 1903.

Year	Name	Country
1980	Joop Zoetemelk	Netherlands
1981	Bernard Hinault	France
1982	Bernard Hinault	France
1983	Laurent Fignon	France
1984	Laurent Fignon	France
1985	Bernard Hinault	France
1986	Greg LeMond	USA
1987	Stephen Roche	Ireland, Republic of
1988	Pedro Delgado	Spain
1989	Greg LeMond	USA
1990	Greg LeMond	USA
1991	Miguel Induráin	Spain
1992	Miguel Induráin	Spain
1993	Miguel Induráin	Spain
1994	Miguel Induráin	Spain
1995	Miguel Induráin	Spain
1996	Bjarne Riis	Denmark
1997	Jan Ullrich	Germany
1998	Marco Pantani	Italy
1999	Lance Armstrong	USA
2000	Lance Armstrong	USA

World Professional Boxing Champions

As of 5 June 2000.
WBA = World Boxing Association; WBC = World Boxing Council; IBF = International Boxing
Federation; WBO = World Boxing Organization.
Weights given are weight limit.

Weight	WBA	WBC	IBF	WBO
Heavyweight (>86.2 kg/>190 lb)	vacant	Lennox Lewis (UK)	Lennox Lewis (UK)	Chris Byrd (USA)
Cruiserweight (86.2 kg/190 lb)	Fabrice Tiozzo (France)	Juan Carlos Gomez (Cuba)	Vasily Jirov (Kazakhstan)	Johnny Nelson (UK)
Light heavyweight (79.4 kg/175 lb)	Roy Jones Jr (USA)	Roy Jones Jr (USA)	Roy Jones Jr (USA)	Darius Michalczewski (Germany)
Super middleweight (76.2 kg/168 lb)	Bruno Girard (France)	Glen Catley (UK)	Sven Ottke (Germany)	Joe Calzaghe (UK)
Middleweight (72.6 kg/160 lb)	William Joppy (USA)	Keith Holmes (USA)	Bernard Hopkins (USA)	Armand Krajne (Slovakia)
Super welterweight (69.9 kg/154 lb)	Felix Trinidad (Puerto Rico)	Javia Castillejo (Spain)	Fernando Vargas (USA)	Harry Simon (Namibia)
Welterweight (66.7 kg/147 lb)	James Page (USA)	Oscar de la Hoya (USA)	vacant	Daniel Santos (USA)
Junior welterweight (63.5 kg/140 lb)	Sharmba Mitchell (USA)	Kostya Tszyu (Russian)	Zab Judah (USA)	Randall Bailey (USA)
Lightweight (61.2 kg/135 lb)	Giberto Serrano (Venezuela)	Steve Johnston (USA)	Paul Spadafora (USA)	Artur Grigorian (Germany)
Junior lightweight (59 kg/130 lb)	Joel Cassamayor (Cuba)	Floyd Mayweather (USA)	Diego Corrales (USA)	Acelino Feitas (Brazil)
Featherweight (57.2 kg/126 lb)	Freddie Norwood (USA)	Guty Espadas (Mexico)	Paul Ingle (UK)	Naseem Hamed (UK)
Junior featherweight (55.3 kg/122 lb)	Bones Adams (USA)	Erik Morales (Mexico)	Lehlohonolo Ledwaba (South Africa)	Mark Antonio Barrera (Mexico)

Weight	WBA	WBC	IBF	WBO
Bantamweight (53.5 kg/118 lb)	Pauli Ayala (USA)	Veerapol Sahaprom (Thailand)	Tim Austin (USA)	Johnny Tapia (USA)
Junior bantamweight (52.2 kg/115 lb)	Hideki Todaka (Japan)	Injoo Choo (South Korea)	vacant	Adonis Rivas (Nicaragua)
Flyweight (50.8 kg/112 lb)	Sornpichai Kratchingdaenggym (Thailand)	Medgoen Z-K Batteryl (Thailand)	Irene Pacheco (Columbia)	Isidro Garcia (USA)
Junior flyweight (49 kg/108 lb)	Pichitnoi Choi Siriwat (Thailand)	Yo-Sam Choi (South Korea)	Ricardo Lopez (Mexico)	Michael Carbajal (USA)
Strawweight (47.6 kg/105 lb)	Noel Arambulet (Venezuela)	Jose Antonio Aguirre (Mexico)	Zolani Petelo (South Africa)	Kermin Guardia (Colombia)

Cricket: World Cup Winners

This competition was first held in 1975.

Year	Winner	Runner-up	Location
1975	West Indies	Australia	England
1979	West Indies	England	England
1983	India	West Indies	England
1987	Australia	England	India
1992	Pakistan	England	Australia
1996	Sri Lanka	Australia	India, Pakistan, and Sri Lanka
1999	Australia	Pakistan	UK